MW00416088

Carnales:

A History of Chicano Vietnam Veterans

By Juan "John" C. Trejo ©2013

~ 2 ~

First Leeds and York Edition

Copyright © 2013

Leeds & York LLC.

ISBN-13: 978-1482061123
ISBN-10: 1482061120

Grateful acknowledgment is made to
Kennesaw State University.
Manufactured in the United States of America

~ 3 ~

This Book is dedicated to all Chicanos and to all those who served in the Vietnam War.

Table of Contents

CHAPTER ONE
THE MIASMA OF THE VIETNAM WAR:
A Historiography of Scholarship on Chicano Vietnam Veterans

During the Cold War the United States became involved in one of the deadliest and most expensive wars in its history. The Vietnam War became a complex situation for the United States who was attempting to institute democracy, and avoid the nation of Vietnam from becoming a communist state. It was an ideological war between communist North Vietnamese soldiers, the Viet Cong and Viet Minh against pro-capitalist and democratic forces composed of the Army of the Republic of Vietnam (ARVN) and U.S. military forces. The forces of the United States were as diverse as the nation of the United States and included soldiers who were from various racial and ethnic backgrounds. Large segments of the US Army, US Navy, US Marines, and US Air-Force were Mexican-American (Chicano), African-American, Native-American, and Asian-American. This literary review aims to focus on discussing the literary works on Chicano soldiers who served in the Vietnam War. The scholarship that has been written on Chicano soldiers and veterans of the war must be analyzed and their contributions must be assessed in order to gain a better understanding of how the Chicano's identity, spirituality, health, political orientation, and overall philosophy regarding life was altered and affected by the Vietnam War.

The use of the term Chicano comes from the history of Chicanos themselves and their Native American Indigenous and Spanish roots. The term refers to a person who is a Mexican-American, and it comes from an accentuated word meaning Mexican. The Nahuatl word mexica was shortened over time to xica and eventually this word was used to refer to Mexican-Americans as Xicanos or Chicanos. The term is different from Hispanic and Latino because those terms refer to notions that are similar but are not exactly the same. In other words Latino refers to people who have roots from the southern European nations like Portugal, France, Spain, and Italy and who were born in the Americas. The word Latino is a Spanish word but could be translated in English as the word Latin, and it refers to people of Latin descent. The term Hispanic can be applied by people who speak Spanish as one of their native languages, or who have ancestors who were of Spanish origin. However the word Chicano refers to people who are Latino and Hispanic but are the descendants of Mexicans and are American citizens. In other words all Chicanos are

Latinos and Hispanics but not all Latinos and Hispanics are Chicanos. Since the southwestern states were lost to the United States during the Mexican-American War of 1846 the term has been used among Mexican-Americans to create a sense of identity and belonging amongst one another. As time has gone by the Chicano ethnic group has grown due to the surges in immigration by Mexicans into the United States.

The Chicano ethnic group can be found all over the United States but the heaviest concentrations of Chicanos have historically been found in the southwest. In theoretical terms the notion of Chicanos becoming a recognized identity by the rest of the United States can be attributed to the years since the 1950s according to Crawford Young. Since the 1950s the terms Chicano and Latino have become a lot more common, especially during the Chicano Civil Rights Movement of the 1960s.[1] There are many commonalities between the ethnic groups that Young references and the Chicano ethnic group. Young states that throughout history Native Americans have been regarded

---

[1] Crawford Young, ed., *The Rising Tide of Cultural Pluralism: The Nation-State at Bay?* (Madison, WI: The University of Wisconsin Press, 1993), 12.

as a savage other by Americans while African-Americans have not been able to enjoy the freedoms and liberties that the Constitution outlined.[2] Chicanos have felt that same degree of discrimination by Anglo-Americans in that they have been regarded as savage others throughout history and they have also experienced segregation from public places such as schools, restaurants, stores, and theatres. It is important to research and discuss how these discriminatory occurrences have affected the perceptions of identity that Chicanos have had. Their participation in the Vietnam War presented problems in their being able to connect with mainstream American culture and society. Using the framework and ideology of Crawford Young the change in Chicano identity because of racial discrimination can be discussed and deciphered.

In the context of the Chicano ethnic group it is also important to discuss the multi-faceted issues that affected Chicano veterans during and after the Vietnam War. The Chicano ethnic group is a collection of historical events and relationships between Indigenous peoples, Spanish peoples, Mexican, and American nationalities. There exists an

[2] Ibid., 28-29.

ethnic hybridity that Gloria Anzaldúa discusses in her book *Borderlands/La Frontera: The New Mestiza* that can be applied not just to queer theory but also to Chicano mestizos. Anzaldúa taps into the issues that affect Chicanos such as discrimination by border fences which deliberately separate Chicanos from Anglo-Americans.[3] She also discusses the difficulties that the Chicano ethnic group has had in adopting the predominant English-only American culture. These theoretical issues can be applied to the research and discussion of Chicano Vietnam War veterans who suffered through difficult times in their attempt of assimilating into English-only American culture and their attempts to be regarded as heroes in a nation that had feelings of hatred and ambiguity towards their existence.

In 1990 Charley Trujillo a Chicano veteran of Vietnam published *Soldados Chicanos in Viet Nam*. His book essentially began the scholarship on the Chicano Vietnam veteran with the essential aim of recording the personal experiences of former war veterans in an uncut and raw fashion. Trujillo stayed away from specific questions regarding the war and instead let the veterans

---

[3] Gloria E. Anzaldúa, *Borderlands/La Frontera: The New Mestiza* (San Francisco, CA: Aunt Lute Books, 1987), 101-103.

discuss their experiences about Vietnam in a very open manner without restrictions. Trujillo simply wrote down what the Chicano veterans described. For example Trujillo interviewed a veteran named Eddie Rodriguez who elaborated on the problems with fighting in the Vietnam War and why it was such a complicated and distorted war. Rodriguez averred that Vietnam felt like a country that was too far away from modern nations like the United States and pointed to things that made him feel as if he was being part of an unethical dictatorship. Rodriguez pointed to in particular prostitute shacks that were made out of wood and cardboard by the Vietnamese to cater to the American soldiers as well as war crimes committed by American soldiers who were attempting to extract information from Viet Cong guerillas.[4] That interview led to a popular theme in Trujillo's book, one that stressed that Chicanos simply wanted to return home and get away from the tragedies and war crimes they experienced in the Vietnam War.

Soldados Chicanos in Viet Nam seemed to stress the confusion that the Vietnam War brought to Chicano soldiers. In another interview that Trujillo conducted with a

---

[4] Charley Trujillo, *Soldados: Chicanos in Viet Nam* (San Jose, CA: Chusma House Publications, 1990), 5-7.

former soldier named Frank Delgado, Delgado described the poor preparation he felt the Army had given him when they briefed him on the Viet Cong. Delgado stated that his superiors had told him that the Viet Cong would be easily recognizable because they wore black pajamas and straw hats but that when he arrived in Saigon the majority of people were dressed in that manner. Like Eddie Rodriguez, Delgado also discussed war crimes he witnessed being committed in Vietnam. Delgado averred that his platoon massacred a Viet Cong soldier while he was in a malaria-induced sleep and that while his lieutenant was astonished at the brutality of the enlisted soldiers he did not send any of them to a court-martial.[5] The themes of war crimes and confusion are predominant in Trujillo's book and this particular scholarly work slightly touches on the fight for a dictatorship. For example in another chapter in which Trujillo interviews former Marine Larry Holguin, Holguin testifies to what he sees as an unpatriotic and un-motivated South Vietnam. Holguin confesses that when he was first sent into Vietnam he believed that the war was a good fight in which the United States was assisting a nation that was

---

[5] Ibid., 17-25.

being encroached upon by communist aggressors and that since the Vietnamese government had requested help in their civil war it was the duty of free nations to help. However he confesses that he eventually realized that he had been brainwashed and lied to by the American government and that he felt that the ARVN soldiers were not willing to fight for democracy or for South Vietnam. Holguin declares that the ARVN forces retreated too easily and that no one who truly believes in what they are fighting for gives up so easily.[6] In his self-testimonial that he incorporated into his book Trujillo himself recalls suffering from the same sort of confusion Holguin came across. He states that once when his platoon was walking through a Vietnamese village they saw an entire platoon of ARVN soldiers playing volleyball and that this experienced made him question how much the soldiers truly cared about the war against the Viet Cong and the North Vietnamese.[7]

The relevant facts that Charley Trujillo's book brings to the discussion of Chicano identity and experience in the Vietnam War are several. Trujillo's book discusses

---

[6] Ibid., 75-77.

[7] Ibid., 155.

the fact that most if not all Chicano soldiers desired to return to their homes in the United States as well as exposing the veterans' experience regarding war crimes. While these accounts describe and discuss these themes it would be important to the research that I desire to conduct to elaborate on how being exposed to those war crimes affected their emotions, their faith and spirituality, and their relationships with their family and other people upon their return to the United States. It would also be important to examine the effects war crimes and the confusion of being in such a controversial war had on their ethnic identities. Questions regarding whether or not they felt more united to Americans of different races and ethnicities given that they had served in a war together should be investigated. Did the war further separate Chicanos from other Americans?

Within a similar context to Charley Trujillo's *Soldados Chicanos in Viet Nam*, Lea Ybarra published a book with accounts by Chicano soldiers titled *Vietnam Veteranos: Chicanos Recall the War*. Ybarra's book explores the carnage and brutality that Chicanos witnessed during the Vietnam War. In an interview Ybarra conducted with an Army veteran named Gilberto, Gilberto recalled that during an intense fire-fight with the North Vietnamese Army they killed as many as three-hundred North Vietnamese. In order to bury the bodies Gilberto recounted that the Army would use bulldozers to dig mass graves.[8] Scenes of inhumanity like these mass graves drove Gilberto to frequently question why America was fighting the Vietnam War, and what he was doing over there.

The question of why Chicanos were fighting in Vietnam and what America was doing in that war is a popular theme among the veterans that Ybarra interviewed. A former US Army Sergeant named Alejandro recalls that during his tour in Vietnam he felt that the Vietnamese people did not want Americans over there and that many civilians and even children were frequently attempting to kill them. He also explains that on one occasion his platoon found American equipment on the Viet Cong and that that made him wonder if some Americans may have been sending supplies to the Viet Cong.[9] This anecdote complements the notions of confusion many Chicano

---

[8] Lea Ybarra, *Vietnam Veteranos: Chicanos Recall the War* (Austin, TX: University of Texas Press, 2004), 19.

[9] Ibid., 39.

soldiers experienced during the war which made many question why they were fighting such an unpopular war. The interview Ybarra conducted with Alejandro also grazes on the difficulties he had finding a job when he returned to America. He explains that he would apply to many factories but that as soon as he told them that he was a Vietnam veteran they would inform him that there were no positions available.

Ybarra's scholarship on the Vietnam War also touches upon the theme of Chicano identity and of how the political feelings of Chicanos were affected by the war. One veteran named Charley discusses that when he returned from the war he was mad at America because he saw that Chicanos at the time made up only ten percent of the population and around thirty percent of the US military personnel. He averred that when he was in Vietnam he did not have a political identity because he felt that America was supporting an authoritarian dictatorship but that when he returned he was willing to risk his life for his Chicano raza (people) and that he took part in Chicano activist causes like the Chicano moratorium.[10] The chapter however

---

[10] Ibid., 45.

concludes with these last words and does not go into depth on what the Chicano moratorium was or why Charley was now so willing to take up political causes. However it must be noted that one thing was for certain regarding many Chicano veterans in Ybarra's book: that their political identities changed once they returned from Vietnam.

In an interview with a former Army soldier named Tony the change in political identity is reaffirmed. Tony comments that it did not take him to long to realize that there was something really wrong and contradictory in Vietnam. He witnessed war crimes and many injustices in the war and upon his return to America he states that he decided to join the Vietnam Veterans against the War. Tony confirms that he felt that the war was being fought for all the wrong reasons and that that's why he decided to take part in many protests against the war.[11] In another case a former Army Sergeant named Raul affirms his change of political identity and his move into intense ethnocentricity because of what the Vietnam War left within him. Raul acknowledges his opposition to communism but he also acknowledges his opposition to the American foreign

---

[11] Ibid., 57.

policy and support of what he viewed as a Vietnamese dictatorship. Most importantly he touches on a few of the reasons why he felt that America was supporting the wrong cause, and alludes to the injustices he saw in Saigon. He remembers that in Saigon there were hundreds of beggars and prostitutes and wondered why would a democratic and just government allow this? These occurrences fomented indignation within Raul and so after the war he enrolled into college and joined the anti-war movement as well as the Movimiento Estudiantil Chicano de Aztlán (MEChA).[12]

Lea Ybarra's *Vietnam Veteranos: Chicanos Recall the War* then jumps to a different theme, one concerning Agent Orange and Post-Traumatic Stress Disorder (PTSD) and what Chicanos experienced regarding these two phenomenon. In an interview with Lupe a former Marine who served in Vietnam the effects of PTSD and Agent Orange were outlined. Lupe states that he was traumatized from seeing one of his fellow Marines being blown to pieces by a child. He recounts that for a long time upon his return to America he had trouble sleeping inside of his family's home and preferred sleeping in the backyard until

---

[12] Ibid., 66-67.

he realized how much his mental difficulties were affecting his mother and then he decided to sleep in the living room. Lupe's emotional and mental difficulties made him turn to alcohol abuse and eventually he ended up living as a homeless person. Lupe attempted suicide three times before finally he realized that he needed help and joined a support group which helped him recover from his traumatic experiences.[13] Within these testimonials it can be inferred that there was dramatic change in the identity of the minds of these Chicano veterans even though it is not detailed or stated outright.

Regarding Agent Orange Ybarra interviews a former Army Corporal named David who discusses his battle with the effects of Agent Orange. David states that the military must have not known of the dangerous effects that Agent Orange produces in human beings because they would constantly spray it to defoliate the Vietnamese jungle while troops were in the area. David confesses that his superiors would lead the soldiers to believe that Agent Orange was really just insecticide to keep the mosquitoes off of the troops. However David explains that years after

---

[13] Ibid., 133-135.

he returned from Vietnam he would get really bad rashes all over his body. The doctors of the Veterans' Administration hospital had no idea what the rashes were from and that eventually it was discovered that it was from the effects of Agent Orange.[14]

Lea Ybarra's book is a very important part of the scholarly work regarding Chicano veterans of the Vietnam War and brings to light many themes regarding the changes in Chicano attitudes and identities regarding the war. It would be important however in my research thesis project to expand on many of the themes that Ybarra's book grazes upon. For example her book mentions the fact that several veterans had trouble finding work after the war and I think that it would be important to ask why did they find it hard to find a job? She also touches on the change in attitudes of Chicanos becoming more politically involved after the war and of Chicanos becoming more aware of their Mexican-American heritage. It would be important to explore why the sudden turn to politics and the awareness of cultural/ethnic identity occurred. The book also explores and testifies to the problems that Chicano veterans had with

---

[14] Ibid., 143-144.

PTSD and Agent Orange and does a good job in documenting some experiences veterans have had with these issues. However it would be important to explore what government and community programs did to address these problems as well as exploring the effects these issues had on Chicano veterans and their families more in depth.

In the exploration regarding how the conflict in Vietnam altered Chicano identities a former US Marine named Juan Ramirez wrote about his experiences in an auto-biography entitled *A Patriot After All: the Story of a Chicano Vietnam Vet.* What was particularly interesting and noteworthy of this literary piece is that Ramirez begins his book by discussing his Mexican-American roots. For example he explains that he is in fact a third generation Chicano and that it was his grandparents that immigrated to the United States in the 1910s. As Mexicans and Mexican-Americans his family was destined to be stuck in the working class and that even though his father Juan Ramirez Sr. at one point raised his family into middle-class status, racism at his father's job resulted in his father losing his job. The loss of Ramirez Sr.'s job along with mental trauma that he suffered from World War II resulted in Ramirez Sr.

resorting to alcohol and a spiral back into the working class.[15] Ramirez discusses how important his extended family was to him and how his religious beliefs helped him through the difficult times he experienced in the war and after the war. When researching the issue of identity in Chicano Vietnam War veterans it is important to understand the family roots of these veterans in order to understand how the war altered their identities. While Ramirez's book was not thorough and does not delve into the core themes that deal with identity, his book does briefly discuss issues that Ybarra and Trujillo merely mention or do not explore.

Two of the main themes that Juan Ramirez explains in his book are the notions of war crimes and the ongoing theme of the confusion Chicano soldiers experienced during Vietnam. He felt confounded by the governmental idea of the strategic hamlet program and stated that it did not feel correct to destroy the homes of the Vietnamese with the idea that one was destroying resources for the Viet Cong. Ramirez especially felt a sense of wrong-doing in

---

[15] Juan Ramirez, *A Patriot After All: the Story of a Chicano Vietnam Vet* (Albuquerque, NM: University of New Mexico Press, 1999), 12-14.

"relocating" the Vietnamese villagers miles away from their homeland.[16] His confusion stemmed from the fact that he wanted to use his participation in the war as a test of his manhood and as an opportunity to achieve honor and glory like other Chicanos had in World War II and in the Korean War, but the war in Vietnam did not seem honorable or glorious to him.

The notion of war crimes in Vietnam becomes a colossal issue for Ramirez as he describes that he witnessed many things that he believed were unjust and out of line. He recalled that he felt like a NAZI by the way soldiers treated Vietnamese civilians. On one occasion he tells of when he was in charge of watching a teenager who was under suspicion of being allied to the Viet Cong. Ramirez knew within himself that the boy as he referred to him was most likely just acting subversive because the American military had burned down his village, and that he sympathized with what the boy was going through. Later the boy ran away while Ramirez was sleeping and another group of marines shot the boy even though the boy was unarmed.[17] This incident sparked extreme indignation

---

[16] Ibid., 42.

within Juan Ramirez and made him question why was he was fighting in Vietnam and how much did the United States truly care about the Vietnamese people. Ramirez reflected that after that tragedy he did not feel like he was truly fighting communism and it seemed that his mind was being flooded by doubts.

Eventually because of his experience and because Ramirez gained the trust and respect of his Lieutenant he was put in charge of a platoon. When he took command of his platoon he created strict rules for his marines because he saw that when soldiers and marines harassed villagers the villagers would lose trust in the American military and would refuse to cooperate with them. He also saw the connection between harassment of villagers and their property and Viet Cong attacks, stating that when villagers or their property were attacked marines and soldiers would get ambushed within a day or two by the Viet Cong. His rules did not put order into his platoon as on one occasion he discovers one of his staff sergeants who was recently added to his platoon trying to rape a Vietnamese girl. He managed to stop the staff sergeant but the damaged had

---

[17] Ibid., 46-48.

already been done the people of the village looked upon the marines with animosity, and by the next day his platoon was ambushed by Vietnamese guerillas.[18] These occurrences that Ramirez experienced in the Vietnam War are important to understand because they are what marked changes in his identity. After the war he becomes a strict opponent of the war and of using military force for invading other nations, and this change in his political identity can be attributed to the war crimes he witnessed.

One of the most important themes that Ramirez outlines in his book that Ybarra and Trujillo do not discuss in detail is the subject of racism in the military and at home that Chicano veterans encountered. He describes his initial squad leader in Vietnam as a racist bigot who did not hesitate to use minority marines in the front line of combat. Jensen, he recalled did not have much time left on his tour in the war and so he would send Ramirez out into the jungle with the rest of the squad while Jensen stayed in the rear area. Ramirez discussed that Jensen used to speak to the Black and Chicano marines using racial epithets and that that made Ramirez question if Jensen even regarded

---

[18] Ibid., 102-104.

the minority soldiers and the Vietnamese villagers as human beings.[19] Later on Jensen ended up risking the lives of his entire squad because of his cowardliness and Ramirez managed to have him removed from command and from the platoon. It is interesting to note how racism played a role in the Vietnam War and how it could be compared to what was occurring in the United States at the time in social history.

Ramirez continues with the theme of racism and describes the institutionalized racism he encountered when he returned to the United States. He reminisced that one night when he was driving a girl on a date a deputy sheriff pulled him over, and because he did not have a driver's license he was arrested. However he did not feel bad for getting arrested he felt that he was pulled over because of the shade of his skin and as Ramirez suspected the deputy was an adamant racist. He averred that the officer shouted racial insults at him and that when he found out that Ramirez was a former marine he questioned his armed service.[20] This incident marks an important issue that

---

[19] Ibid., 64-65.

[20] Ibid., 90-91.

affects all Chicanos and that is the issue of being racially profiled by the police, and of being viewed as a second class citizen whose contributions to American history are regarded as meaningless.

Juan Ramirez's book deals with important issues regarding Chicano veterans of the Vietnam War. He discusses war crimes, his heritage, racism, his confusion and doubts of the war, and his struggle upon arriving home with drugs and unemployment. His scholarship contributes quite a bit of information to the study of Chicano identity and its change from the Vietnam War but more research could be added to his work. For example it would be important to explore the connections between the war crimes Chicano veterans experienced and how those experiences affected their views of spirituality, identity, and armed conflicts. It would also be interesting to search for the connection between Chicano heritage and the sense of belonging in American society. In other words did the participation of Mexican-Americans in the war create a sense of belonging in American society? How did their Chicano heritage play a part in how Chicano veterans viewed the war before and after their participation in it?

Additional research in this field could possibly explain some of the notions of identity regarding Chicano veterans. For example Ramirez discusses his increased interest in being involved in issues that affect the Mexican-American community after his participation in the war; it would be important to contribute to this field of study the reasons why many Chicanos wanted to get in touch with their ethnic brothers.

Adding to the scholarship that has been written regarding the Chicano experience in the Vietnam War, Gil Dominguez a former Vietnam veteran wrote *They Answered the Call: Latinos in the Vietnam War*. His book incorporated an enormous amount of interviews that he conducted with Chicano war veterans in the attempt to prove that Mexican-Americans have contributed quite a great deal of sacrifice to American military service. While his book seemed to focus mainly on the battles that Chicanos engaged in Dominguez inadvertently discusses and mentions the identities of Chicano veterans.

In his book Dominguez interviewed twenty-one Latino veterans of which eighteen were Mexican-Americans. In his recollection of the lives of these Chicano veterans it can be concluded that the majority of them came from impoverished backgrounds, single-parent homes, and that they indeed had no other choice but to either be drafted into the military or volunteer for service. For example Dominguez interviews a Chicano Vietnam veteran who describes his youth as a game of survival recalling that he had grown up in the infamous Victoria Courts neighborhood in San Antonio, Texas. The veteran named Jack White stated that his father passed away before White could graduate from high school which forced White to drop-out of school in order to provide for his mother, sister, and brother. Without a job that paid a wage that they could live off of White confessed that he had no other choice but to join the Navy in 1963.[21] While not all of Chicano Vietnam veterans came from poverty stricken backgrounds it seems to be a recurring theme in the works of Ybarra, Ramirez, Trujillo, and Dominguez. In his book Dominguez does not go into detail about his interviewees' background, in most cases only allotting one page but he does make sure to mention that many Chicano veterans had little choice in what to do during the war.

---

[21] Gil Dominguez, *They Answered the Call: Latinos in the Vietnam War* (Baltimore, MD: Publish America, 2004), 58.

In another example Dominguez describes the childhood of Antonio Bustamante who grew up in a housing project in the Westside of San Antonio. Bustamante confessed that he never knew who his father was and that his mother remarried an abusive man. When Bustamante graduated from high school having no money or scholarships to go to college he decided to join the Marine Corps.[22] This theme of living in poverty and broken families becomes a major part of identity in Chicano Vietnam veterans. Even though Dominguez mentions some of these issues that drove Mexican-Americans into joining the military more could be added to the scholarship and research of this subject. The factors that came together in the United States that led many Chicanos to live in poverty must be examined for example institutionalized racism, the revolving cycle of poverty, and the priorities in Chicano culture. In other words is education a priority for Mexican-Americans when their financial stability is in danger? Is putting food on the table of their homes more important than waiting for a future degree that may or may not provide better employment? Those are the factors that

---

[22] Ibid., 72.

relate to Chicano identity that need to be further elaborated on.

Living in a nation as a member of an ethnic minority can have a great effect on identity. The effects can be feelings of non-belonging caused by racism and feelings of animosity towards the major ethnicity. The theme of racism and of feeling as a minority or as an outsider becomes a theme that Dominguez also discusses however in his attempt to sketch all Chicano veterans as heroes, Dominguez does not excavate deep enough into the problem of racism as it affects identity. His book nonetheless does mention important racist events that occurred in the lives of Chicano Vietnam veterans that shaped who they became. For example a former Army veteran named Juan Jose Peña averred that he had collisions with institutionalized racism since he was in elementary school. Peña recalled that his teachers in elementary school prohibited his use of the Spanish language and referred to Chicano students as those "stupid Mexicans." Peña discussed that racism was just as bad in the military as it was in his days in school and recalled that although he made sergeant he could never become a senior non-commissioned officer because he was Hispanic.[23] In the study of identity regarding Chicano Vietnam veterans it would be important to research how Mexican-American veterans felt neglected in their military service because of their ethnicity. Dominguez brushes on some of the experiences that occurred to these veterans but does not go into detail about how that affected their identities. In other words how did racism in the military affect the binary of discrimination and patriotism in the Chicano veteran? Another question to be asked would be how did racism affect the Chicano veterans' behavior or personal characteristics? Both of these questions need to be answered in the study of veteran identity change.

The third major theme that Dominguez discusses in his book is the notion of religion and spiritual beliefs. Religion and spiritual beliefs plays an important component in the identity of Chicanos, and in order to research and discuss how the Vietnam War affected the identity of Mexican-American veterans, religion must be a point of focus. In his book Dominguez interviews a veteran named Mike Serrano who describes his indignation towards the

---

[23] Ibid., 164-165.

Catholic Church. Serrano reminisces about a time that a fellow soldier and him killed a Viet Cong guerilla and declares that the incident affected his spirituality severely. After having nightmares about the incident, Serrano went to talk about it with the Catholic priest back at base. Serrano confronted the priest asking him why Catholic soldiers were given blessings if they were going out to kill, a sin that is denounced within the Ten Commandments, but the priest told him that it was essentially okay because they were going out to kill Communists. Communists the priest described, were enemies of God, and so it was his Christian duty to carry out God's wrath.[24] Serrano recalls that he felt that that was not a satisfactory answer and that although he never abandoned his Catholic beliefs, he grew disappointed and disillusioned with the Catholic clergy. Religion plays an integral part in the identity of a Mexican-American as the majority of the population is Christian, and most of them are Roman Catholic but war can have devastating effects on how people perceive spirituality. It would be an important part of the study of the identity of Chicano veterans to delve into more examples of how spirituality

---

[24] Ibid., 128-129.

was perceived and changed by the Vietnam War. In Catholic doctrine there exist too many ideas that contradict going to war or taking part in wars against other human beings, and it would be important to analyze how Chicanos felt about these contradictions.

The last major theme that Gil Dominguez touches upon that relates to identity is political affiliation and personal political philosophy. In an interview with former soldier George Bielma who served in the Vietnam War the binary of pride and humiliation is discussed in short detail. Bielma describes that in the middle of his tour of duty in Vietnam he realized that the U.S. government was using Mexican-Americans as cannon fodder. He averred that he saw that the government was disproportionately recruiting Chicanos and African-Americans into the military especially with their urban youth program that lowered the standards in the Armed Forces Qualifying Test so that more impoverished men could go to Vietnam. Bielma admitted that when he first joined the military he believed in the fight against communism and was very patriotic but that when he returned from the war he saw it as a waste of human lives and came to hate the government of America.[25]

Bielma's testimony brings to the forefront the importance of personal political philosophy in its relationship with identity. Although Dominguez does not go into great detail about how or why the political affiliation of Chicano veterans seemed to change after the Vietnam War it is imperative in this subject area to understand why Chicano veterans tended to leave conservatism towards more radical ideas.

George Mariscal's book *Aztlán and Viet Nam: Chicano and Chicana Experiences of the War*, outlines two of the main themes concerning Chicano veterans' identity during and after the Vietnam War. Mariscal's book does not completely focus on Chicano veterans but it does contain poems and testimonials written by Chicano veterans that describe their experiences in the war. One of the main themes that Mariscal discusses is the notion of racism that Chicano veterans experienced during their military service. In one example Leroy V. Quintana a former veteran writes in a poem within the book that his high school graduation day was a grand affair that did not include any college recruiters. Quintana describes a

---

[25] Ibid., 121.

graduation day filled with armed forces recruiters from every military branch instead, and that that made him feel that the American government did not want Chicanos in college but in Vietnam instead.[26] Quintana's poem underlines the notion of using Mexican-Americans as front-line infantrymen and ignoring their desire to become something more beneficial to society than cannon-fodder.

In another example of racism in Mariscal's book the experiences of a Chicano Vietnam veteran named Octavio I. Romano is discussed. Romano recalls being back in California on leave before going to Vietnam. In the incident Romano gets pulled over by a police officer who pulled him over just because he looked Hispanic. Romano was with his Irish-American girlfriend and states that he was targeted by the police because he was a Mexican-American with a white girlfriend.[27] After this embarrassing incident with the police Romano left to serve in the Vietnam War which brings up the dichotomy of being hated and being a

---

[26] George Mariscal, *Aztlán and Viet Nam: Chicano and Chicana Experiences of the War* (Berkeley, CA: University of California Press, 1999), 81.

[27] Ibid., 169.

war hero at the same time. While Mariscal only mentions a few incidents of racism geared towards Chicano war veterans it would be important to add more research as to how racism affected Chicano veterans and how it affected their personal characteristics.

The second theme that Mariscal's book deals with that is pertinent to the study of identity as it relates to Chicano Vietnam War veterans is the confusion Chicanos experienced in the war. For example Everett Alvarez, Jr. discusses how he began to see the war in Vietnam no longer as a war to free the world against communism but as a war that supported a dictatorship and capitalist companies. Alvarez described South Vietnam as one coup d'état after another in an incomprehensible swirl of political corruption, and came to the conclusion that if Buddhist monks were willing to burn themselves in protest something was not right about the pretended goals of the war.[28] In another chapter of Mariscal's book a Chicano war veteran wrote a letter to describe what he saw as futile about the war in Vietnam. Ignacio Garcia declared that if the war was like a soccer game and taking lives were like

---

[28] Ibid., 130.

goals scored the United States would have already won, but the war is not like soccer it is about motivation and drive. Garcia states that American soldiers do not have the amount of motivation and drive that the communist Vietnamese soldiers have. The Vietnamese communists have waged this war for over thirty years and did not demonstrate any signs of giving up the fight.[29] The confusion that Mariscal discusses in his book regarding the reasons for the war is important in the study of Chicano identity. However it is imperative to discuss how Chicanos viewed the communist Vietnamese. Where there similarities in these two different groups of people or did Chicanos simply see the Vietnamese as different? How did the confusion in the Vietnam War affect how Chicanos saw their country's leadership? Exploring these questions would help to better understand how Mexican-Americans changed because of the war.

Lorena Oropeza a specialist in Chicano history and a professor at the University of California, Davis, presents different themes that relate to how Chicano identity changed because of the Vietnam War. Oropeza discusses

---

[29] Ibid., 134.

the notion of warrior-hood as a means of Americanization. In her book *Raza Si! Guerra No! Chicano Protest and Patriotism During the Viet Nam War Era* Oropeza outlines the contributions of Mexican-American soldiers since World War I. The book argues that since Chicanos are both Mexican and American, Indigenous and European, they are caught in a society in which they must try to conform to both cultures. One way of becoming accepted into the dominant English-speaking culture for Chicanos has been through their participation in foreign wars. However Oropeza questions how much acceptance Chicanos have gained through their participation in military service. In one example she depicts two occasions in which American patriotism was celebrated in Lockhart and Poteet, Texas where all people of Spanish descent were asked to leave.[30] Despite being banned from several patriotic celebrations and by being segregated from the Anglo-American population Hispanics continued to enlist and be drafted into the military. Oropeza states that Chicanos had developed a culture of warrior-hood by the time the Vietnam War took

---

[30] Lorena Oropeza, *Raza Si! Guerra No! Chicano Protest and Patriotism During the Viet Nam War Era* (Berkeley, CA: University of California Press, 2005), 14.

place, and saw participation in the unpopular war as a rite of passage and as a test of Chicano machismo. Her discussion on warrior-hood as a means of Americanization for Chicano veterans is revolutionary in the subject area of Chicano identity, but Oropeza could have added how warrior-hood affected the identity of returning Chicano Vietnam veterans. The question that needed to be answered was did Chicanos feel more Americanized when they returned from the war? Instead her book diverts in a different direction focusing on the protests that took place in Los Angeles, CA by the Brown Berets and the Chicano moratorium marches.

Oropeza's book also discusses a theme that affected Mexican-Americans during their participation in the Vietnam War that dealt with the connection she tried to make regarding American Imperialism and the American domestic policy of manifest destiny. Oropeza steps into a problematic idea of trying to relate American interventionism in Vietnam to the American idea of manifest destiny in the North American continent.[31] While there were similarities in the conquering of Mexican and

---

[31] Ibid., 100-101.

Native American lands when American expansionism was coming into fruition a scholar cannot state that Chicanos and the Vietnamese were the same groups of people simply because their skin colors were alike. Such a claim is problematic and can be offensive because the two ethnic and racial groups lived a different language, different beliefs, and different circumstances. However Oropeza does bring about an important point in that she tries to show how one dominant military force conquered the west and a century later tried conquering Southeast Asia, even though it first desired land and in the latter it desired an idea. It would be beneficial to the scholarship and research dealing with Chicano veteran identity to determine how these connections affected Chicanos who served in the Vietnam War. In other words: did the similarities between manifest destiny and American interventionism affect the Mexican-American identity of Chicano soldiers? How did Chicanos view the war on communism in Vietnam?

The other popular theme that many scholars discuss when they deal with the subject of Mexican-American involvement in the war in Vietnam is racism. Oropeza discusses racism as one of the chief notions in her book but discusses it in a limited manner as it relates to Vietnam veterans. For example she alludes to a letter an anonymous Marine of Hispanic descent wrote to a more radical newspaper in which he discussed how racism was prevalent in the armed forces. The Marine regretted going to the war in Vietnam and felt that it was not a war that Hispanics should have been involved in because they were being treated like animals in combat zones and in the United States.[32] Oropeza's anecdote is meaningful to the dialogue of Chicano veteran identity but it is her sole example in her book that deals with racism towards Vietnam veterans of Hispanic descent. It is imperative that more be discussed regarding how racism played a role in shaping the identity and behavior of Mexican-American veterans during and after the war. A history must be written about some of these incidents so that the time and circumstances of the war can be better understood.

Another important theme in discussing how identity was changed by the Vietnam War in Chicano veterans is the issue of approval of the war. In an article entitled "Race, Casualties, and Opinion in the Vietnam War,"

---

[32] Ibid., 109.

which appeared in *The Journal of Politics*, the issues of approval of the war and of Mexican-American patriotism came to the forefront. What Scott Sigmund Gartner and Gary M. Segura discovered in their research was that in the early years of the war, Chicanos approved of the war in large proportions and at some points even higher than conservative Anglo-Americans.[33] This piece of information and data could help scholars understand why many Mexican-Americans volunteered to go to Vietnam instead of waiting to be drafted.

Gartner and Segura present data that is essential to the study of the Chicano approval and disapproval of the war at various times in history, and mention that the differences in approval between Anglo-Americans and Mexican-Americans must be related to characteristics in ethnicity. They mention that Chicanos are very patriotic and that the fight against communism may have played with their feelings regarding the dominant Catholic faith of the Mexican-American community.[34] In one particular

---

[33] Scott Sigmund Gartner and Gary M. Segura, "Race, Casualties, and Opinion in the Vietnam War," *The Journal of Politics* No. 1, Vol. 62 (Feb., 2000): 120.

[34] Ibid., 121.

sentence they argue that perhaps the year 1968 marked the point that Chicanos began opposing the war more heavily along with climbing Chicano casualty rates. Gartner and Segura reference the TET Offensive and the assassination of Robert Kennedy, a popular politician in the Mexican-American community, as watershed events in the war approval rates of Chicanos.[35]

The most important idea that this article contributes to the amassment of historical work composed on Chicano participation in the Vietnam War and Mexican-American identity is discussing how high casualty rates amounted to a decline in approval for the war. However a few ideas and notions need to be further elaborated, for example the connection between ethnic characteristics and approval and disapproval of the war. The tenets of Roman Catholic doctrine could be discussed as many Mexican-American soldiers were adherents of this religion. How did Chicanos deal with the conflicting binary of being prohibited to kill another person while at the same time encouraged to fight communism because of its negative views of religion? Another characteristic that could have caused their

---

[35] Ibid., 124.

vicissitudes in approval of the conflict would be the history of Mexican-Americans to notions of invasion and conquest. The history of a Mexican-American comes from two different worlds, the world of the Native Americans and the world of European influence, and a history of manifest destiny and Spanish colonization. It is a paramount point to discuss how these anecdotes of history influenced Chicano veterans' perceptions of the Vietnam War and how they affected their identity. Gartner and Segura touch on machismo and patriotism as two characteristics that set Mexican-Americans apart from other racial and ethnic groups in the United States during this period, and those two characteristics must be examined as well.

In dealing with the themes of machismo and patriotism comes another scholar named John Alba Cutler into the limelight of Chicano veteran identity during the Vietnam War era. In his article "Disappeared Men: Chicana/o Authenticity and the American War in Viet Nam," Cutler recognizes that the Mexican-American literature and history regarding the war are indeed very limited. Cutler states that the history and literature of Chicanos in the Vietnam War is limited, because machismo and what he calls warrior masculinity has worked against the production of scholarship and instead has advocated for warrior patriotism.[36] In other words many Mexican-American veterans and scholars want to remember their participation in military conflicts which include the Vietnam War as a part of their history as the quintessential patriots. Even though Cutler's article deals more with instances of machismo in fictional Chicano narratives of the war the theme that he brings to the forefront is important to discuss in the study of Chicano identity as affected by the Vietnam War. How warrior masculinity and patriotism affected the characteristics of Mexican-Americans during and after the war is important to research in order to gain a true understanding of how identity was affected.

---

[36] John Alba Cutler, "Disappeared Men: Chicana/o Authenticity and the American War in Viet Nam," *American Literature* No. 3, Vol. 81 (Sept. 2009): 586.

References

Anzaldúa, Gloria E. *Borderlands/La Frontera: The New Mestiza.* San Francisco, CA: Aunt Lute Books, 1987.

Cutler, John Alba. "Disappeared Men: Chicana/o Authenticity and the American War in Viet Nam." *American Literature* no. 3, vol. 81 (September 2009): 583-611.

Dominguez, Gil. *They Answered the Call: Latinos in the Vietnam War*. Baltimore, MD: Publish America, 2004.

Gartner, Scott Sigmund and Gary M. Segura. "Race, Casualties, and Opinion in the Vietnam War." *The Journal of Politics* no. 1, vol. 62 (February 2000): 115-146.

Mariscal, George. *Aztlán and Viet Nam: Chicano and Chicana Experiences of the War*. Berkeley, CA: University of California Press, 1999.

Oropeza, Lorena. *Raza Si! Guerra No! Chicano Protest and Patriotism During the Viet Nam War Era*. Berkeley, CA: University of California Press, 2005.

Ramirez, Juan. *A Patriot After All: the Story of a Chicano Vietnam Vet*. Albuquerque, NM: University of New Mexico Press, 1999.

Trujillo, Charley. *Soldados: Chicanos in Viet Nam.* San Jose, CA: Chusma House Publications, 1990.

Ybarra, Lea. *Vietnam Veteranos: Chicanos Recall the War.* Austin, TX: University of Texas Press, 2004.

Young, Crawford. *The Rising Tide of Cultural Pluralism: The Nation-State at Bay?* Madison, WI: The University of Wisconsin Press, 1993.

CHAPTER TWO

GUERILLEROS:

The Vietnam War and its Effects on Chicano Identity

For generations there has existed an ethnic group in the United States that refers to themselves as Mexican-Americans or Chicanos. The first group of Mexican-Americans to be referred to as such were the Mexican citizens of the states of Texas, New Mexico, California, and all of the other lands that Mexico lost in the Mexican-American War of 1846. Before these lands were lost by Mexico these Mexican-Americans were Mexican, and before Mexico gained its independence from Spain they were Spanish citizens of New Spain. After the Mexican-American War many Mexicans refused to leave their ancestral lands and became American citizens under the Treaty of Guadalupe Hidalgo of 1848. Since that time Chicanos have referred to themselves as Mexican-Americans or Chicanos, and these terms include the sons of Mexican immigrants who are born in the United States. Chicanos sometimes refer to themselves as Latinos or Hispanics, but these are terms that describe how Chicanos fit into the much larger community of peoples from Spanish-speaking nations or nations where a Latin culture was adopted. In other words all Chicanos are Hispanic and Latino but not all Hispanics and Latinos are Chicanos.

Latino refers to any person who descends from a Latin nation, and thus includes Portuguese-speaking peoples from Brazil and Italian-speaking Argentines.

The term Chicano has been a popular term in use since the Chicano Movement of the 1960s and has its origins in the Nahuatl word for Mexico. Today many Mexican-Americans embrace the term as a word that creates unity between all Mexican-Americans, however other Mexican-Americans prefer to use terms that describe what state they are from like Tejano, Californio, and Nuevomexicano. Sandra Cisneros helped to develop the idea of Chicano and Chicana as terms to identify Mexican-Americans in her book *Woman Hollering Creek and Other Stories*.[37] In this essay the terms Chicano and Mexican-American will be used frequently to signify the brotherhood or *carnalismo* that exists within this ethnic group.

Mexican-Americans have had a difficult time gaining acceptance from the rest of American society. The differences in language, culture, and customs have set Chicanos apart from other European-Americans who have

---

[37] Sandra Cisneros, *Woman Hollering Creek and Other Stories* (New York, NY: Vintage/Random House, 1992).

assimilated into the dominant English speaking culture. Time and time again Chicanos have attempted to become a part of this English speaking American society by joining the military falling into the philosophy that states that if one is willing to die for a nation then one is a de facto member of that nation. The Chicano fights an identity battle within himself that he brings out to the physical world in the effort of demonstrating to himself and to American society that he is worthy. Within himself is the battle of being an Indigenous person and at the same time being a descendant of Spain and other parts of Europe, because he is not a simple person he is a complex individual. This binary of identity becomes even more complex when the dichotomy of being of Mexican descent and American-born is factored into the discussion of Chicano identity.

The notion of craving acceptance into the English dominant American societal complex for Chicanos was well exemplified during the Vietnam War. The Vietnam War was for the Chicano an opportunity to fight for America the land of his birth, and an opportunity to be a warrior for democracy and capitalism the ideals that the United States was promoting. For many young Chicanos with no real prospects of obtaining a quality college education or a job the war and joining the military seemed to ostensibly be a route to earn money for a more promising future. However the war proved to be controversial, unpopular, and traumatic for most of the Mexican-American soldiers and sailors that participated in it. Several factors in the understanding of their identities were changed, and their behavioral and cultural characteristics as well as their ethnic understanding of themselves were also altered by the war. This essay seeks to demonstrate how Chicano identity was changed by the Vietnam War, and what particular characteristics were altered.

America's involvement in the war can be traced as far back to President Harry S. Truman's administration. Truman supported France in Vietnam's war for colonial independence from France and lower-level functionaries of his administration met with Ngo Dinh Diem and his brother.[38] Diem would eventually become the president of Vietnam in 1955 with the support of President Dwight D. Eisenhower. The year before Diem's ascent to the

---

[38] Seth Jacobs, *America's Miracle Man in Vietnam: Ngo Dinh Diem, Religion, Race, and U.S. Intervention in Southeast Asia, 1950-1957* (Durham, NC: Duke University Press, 2004), 27.

presidency Vietnam had won its war of independence against France and was subsequently divided into two separate countries: Communist North Vietnam and an ostensibly democratic republic of South Vietnam. Ho Chi Minh and the North Vietnamese government were not satisfied with the terms of the treaty and desired to unify all of Vietnam as one country even if it meant unification by force. President Eisenhower feared that if nations began to fall under communist rule their fall would produce a domino effect. Since countries were under communist rule in Europe and Asia he believed it was only a matter of time before communist rebels and activists would be successful in the Americas. Eisenhower sent economic aid and weapons to South Vietnam. His successor John F. Kennedy would eventually add 16,500 military advisors to the American effort to fight a communist takeover in Vietnam.[39] It seemed that the United States was completely submerged into the struggle for who would control Vietnam.

---

[39] Michael Nelson, ed., *The Evolving Presidency: Addresses, Cases, Essays, Letters, Reports, Resolutions, Transcripts, and Other Landmark Documents, 1787-1998* (Washington, DC: Congressional Quarterly Inc., 1999), 170.

Mexican-Americans became targets of the military in terms of the draft. Unintentionally or not Chicanos had very limited arguments and chances of not being conscripted into the military or of fleeing the country to avoid the war. Due to the poorer state of public education in areas where Hispanics resided, most Chicanos did not enroll into colleges and universities and therefore had more limited chances of obtaining a draft deferment. Hispanic young men were heavily recruited or drafted after they graduated from high school and even if they dropped out. At predominantly Hispanic schools military recruiters and ROTC programs were the answer for escaping the barrio for many Chicanos.[40] That escape however came at an expensive price and for many the price was death, but for those who survived the war physical and mental problems as well as changes in their identities became a common phenomenon.

The identity of Mexican-Americans who enlisted or were drafted into the military and served in the Vietnam War changed in many ways. One way that identity was

---

[40] Mario T. García and Sal Castro, *Blowout! Sal Castro & the Chicano Struggle for Educational Justice* (Chapel Hill, NC: The University of North Carolina Press, 2011), 122-123.

altered by the war was through the relationships that these veterans had with their family members. In the Mexican-American culture the social concept of family is heavily endorsed and emphasized. As many Chicanos adhere to Roman Catholicism and other forms of Christianity, the family unit has become the central social relationship in that culture. The tenets of Catholicism and Christianity outline what a person should live his life by, and being monogamous and being a good father or mother is a central notion in that doctrine.

Juan Ramirez in his book *A Patriot After All: the Story of a Chicano Vietnam Vet* demonstrates how important his family was to him before he joined the military. He states that his grandmother who was of Indigenous descent was the most important person in his life. After all the troubles that he would eventually go through from having served in the Vietnam War, her faith and her teachings to him would be what helped him overcome the issues that were created within him because of the war.[41] In his biography Ramirez discusses that the

---

[41] Juan Ramirez, *A Patriot After All: the Story of a Chicano Vietnam Vet* (Albuquerque, NM: University of New Mexico Press, 1999), 6-7.

violence, war crimes, and brutality that he experienced in the war distorted and became an obstacle in having a good relationship with his family.

The barbarous nature of the war left great psychological wounds in Chicano veterans. It can be inferred that the violence against other human beings made it difficult for veterans to surpass seeing their own family in a non-hostile manner. Marcello, an Army veteran who chose not to give his last name and who served as a First Lieutenant as a Forward Observer, commented on the brutality that he stated injured his ability to feel. Marcello averred that many soldiers grew numb to the violence and would stack dead enemy corpses one on top of the other as if they were nothing. The worst was that many of the Viet Cong that were killed were women, and soldiers would stack dead women on top of dead men as if they were fornicating.[42] Like many other Chicanos who returned from the war Marcello eventually divorced his wife, because she felt that he was no longer the person that he used to be. He confessed that he knew he was not the same person he was when he married her, and that his issues with anxiety and

---

[42] Lea Ybarra, *Vietnam Veteranos: Chicanos Recall the War* (Austin, TX: University of Texas Press, 2004), 167.

depression were definitely caused by the war.[43] The violent behavior of soldiers that found themselves in desperate situations, and of the effects of booby-traps set by the North Vietnamese Army (NVA) and the Viet Cong can be attributed as one of the main reasons why Chicanos had trouble adapting to the social concept of family.

The lack of communication during the war between Chicanos and their families was also a voluminous issue that affected relationships with family members. The 1960s were not a time in which fast communication was in place, and the telephone systems that did exist were not within reach of soldiers that were patrolling the jungles of Vietnam. In a way for many soldiers home became a place that was out of reach and beyond the horizon, and writing letters became a form of momentary escape from the perils of war. However because of the anti-war movement in the United States many soldiers would write letters home and receive no letters back. On several occasions soldiers would strive to make it out of Vietnam alive to be reunited with their girlfriends only to find out that she was no longer interested in dating a Vietnam War veteran.[44]

---

[43] Ybarra, 170.

The notion of relationships with family members presents a complicated and varied reality for Chicano veterans. In some ways strong familial ties were what helped Mexican-Americans transcend the violent occurrences of the war. Luis Muñiz Lopez an Army veteran of Vietnam declared that if it was not for his wife and children back in America he would not have made it out of the war alive. Lopez stated that he would write letters to his wife at every chance that he would have, and that his wife would record her voice and the voices of their children on tapes that she would mail to him.[45] He never divorced her and he averred that he loved her until the day she died. However, every circumstance may be different depending on the person as Lopez stated that he had a very strong connection to his family before he left for war.[46] His mentality and his identity with his family were strong enough to overcome the traumas of the war. For many

---

[44] Gil Dominguez, *They Answered the Call: Latinos in the Vietnam War* (Baltimore, MD: Publish America, 2004), 89.

[45] Lopez, Luis Muñiz. 2009. Interview by William L. Browne. August 7. Transcript, Veterans History Project, The Library of Congress, Washington, DC.

[46] Lopez.

Chicanos however the degree of violence and degradation that they experienced in Vietnam did have drastic effects on how they perceived and related to family members.

For many Chicanos joining the military was part of the beliefs that were indoctrinated into them by their families. As Mexican-Americans the history of warrior-hood has survived to the twentieth century and beyond. A Chicano lives with his mestizo history of having roots to Aztec, Tarascan, or Apache warriors as well as his connection to the Spanish conquistador. The idea of proving oneself through participation in combat is a notion that has been passed down through generations. As Lorena Oropeza stated in her book *¡Raza Si! ¡Guerra No! Chicano Protest and Patriotism During the Viet Nam War Era*, in leading up to the Vietnam War Mexican-Americans could boast that they had earned more Medals of Honor than any other ethnic group during World War II and the Korean War.[47] The idea of joining the military and ostensibly fighting for the safety of one's country, beliefs, and family resonate well in the minds of Chicanos. However the

---

[47] Lorena Oropeza, *¡Raza Si! ¡Guerra No! Chicano Protest and Patriotism During the Viet Nam War Era* (Berkeley, CA: University of California Press, 2005), 54.

Vietnam War turned out to be different as many were misled about the reality of the conflict, and what the United States government was really supporting.

Regarding the discourse of Chicano identity and how it was changed due to the conflict in Vietnam another notion besides family comes to the forefront that is part of Mexican-American identity and that is the notion of patriotism. In other words how proud were Chicanos about being American and what motivated them to join the military? This debate counters ideas brought about by more conservative thinkers like Samuel Huntington, who in his article *The Hispanic Challenge* accuses Chicanos and other Hispanics of being the single most immediate danger to America's traditional identity. Huntington declares that Black and White Americans are native to the United States giving an understanding that Chicanos and other Hispanics are not natives to America.[48] However it is false to believe that Mexican-Americans are not part of the English-speaking American culture and it can be discerned that many felt it was their patriotic duty to enlist into the military during the Vietnam War.

[48] Samuel P. Huntington, "The Hispanic Challenge," *Foreign Policy* no. 141 (March-April 2004): 32.

Patriotism and poverty were two important factors in the identity of Chicanos that led many to enlist into the military during the war. Ralph Garcia a former Marine stated that he decided to enlist into the Marine Corps because he saw that they were the toughest, and that if he wanted to be as tough as they were he had to prove himself by joining. He also recalled that when he was twelve years old he saw a Chicano Marine walking through his barrio in the blue dress uniform returning from the Korean War. Garcia saw how patriotic he looked and he felt that in order to be somebody of importance he had to join the Marines.[49] Garcia embodies the patriotism of wanting to belong to something and to feel a part of something larger than himself.

Garcia was not alone in volunteering to join the military, nor was enlisting in the military an occurrence unique to American-born Chicanos. Manuel Marin was a Mexican who entered the United States illegally and who after being granted his permanent residency or "green card" felt that it was his duty as a Mexican-American to serve in

---

[49] Garcia, Ralph. 2002. Interview by Philip Shaull. December 17. Transcript, Veterans History Project, The Library of Congress, Washington, DC.

the military. Marin joined the Navy and stated that he had to give something back to the country where he had lived in for most of his life. He affirmed that he wanted to go to college like his Anglo-American friends but that he was poor, and that his chances of going to college were scarce.[50] However Marin and other Chicano veterans like him affirm the strong sense of patriotism that existed in the Mexican-American community during the earlier stages of the war. Many Mexican-Americans saw that Vietnam would be their chance to prove to other racial and ethnic groups of their country that they were also proud of being American and that they were willing to make the ultimate sacrifice of dying in combat. Chicanos also desired to prove to their predecessors who had fought valiantly in World War I, World War II, and the Korean War that they were as patriotic and as macho as they were.

The war in Vietnam however caused a rift in that averred patriotism by its exploitation of the Chicano soldier and its use of soldiers as cannon fodder in a confusing and aimless conflict. President Lyndon Johnson declared that the war in Vietnam was a war in which communism had to

[50] Charley Trujillo, *Soldados: Chicanos in Viet Nam* (San Jose, CA: Chusma House Publications, 1990), 41.

be contained, but many soldiers declared that after several weeks in combat they did not understand the purpose of the United States in Vietnam. The notion of confusion became popular in the military fronts and patrols in the jungles of Vietnam, and it created a state of entropy among the soldiers.

Mike Serrano came to embody the confusion that many Mexican-Americans experienced during the war. Serrano stated that his naïveté and romanticisms of the war as a great crusade against the evils of communism came to a halt. He did not care about saving the Vietnamese people anymore; he only cared about making it through his tour of duty alive. Serrano grew to call himself an animal because he only wanted to survive not caring about anything else.[51] Due to the fact that the United States had nebulous reasons for being involved in Vietnam many Chicano soldiers lost morale along with their humanity. Juan Ramirez remembers the exact time when he lost his morale and confusion about his involvement in the war grew. Ramirez was serving in Quang Nam Province in January of 1969 when he came to the realization that he was not

----

[51] Dominguez, 127.

accomplishing his goal. Ramirez believed that to fight communism was a noble goal but grew confused because nothing that he was experiencing felt like he or the military were fighting communism. All he saw was the destruction of the lives and property of the Vietnamese people and the support of a dictatorship.[52]

The sense of patriotism that Chicanos had before their participation in the war in Vietnam was altered by their experiences in the conflict. The destruction that they witnessed and at times inflicted on the Vietnamese villagers created a sense of confusion regarding why America was involved in the civil war between North and South Vietnam. For many Chicanos who survived the war the violence, destruction, and confusion of the war led to animosity or indifference towards government. Robert a former Marine Corps Sergeant embodies the tension toward government by stating that Vietnam was a war that could not be won. Robert admits that if he knew then what he knows now he would have never gone to the war, because it was a situation where American kids were dying every day and there was no clear objective.[53] Many Chicanos

[52] Ramirez, 50-51.

returned from the war with the same feelings, and they were not necessarily feelings of anti-patriotism. Rather the feelings that Mexican-Americans felt upon their return to America were sentiments that government cannot be blindly trusted.

The hostility and fear that Chicanos felt towards government upon their return from the war was not new to Mexican-Americans, but it was surprising that the United States acted in a controversial manner. For many Chicanos that were aware of their Mexican roots a corrupt and dictatorial government was to be hated. In Mexico Porfirio Díaz and the Institutionalized Revolutionary Party (PRI) were the root causes of Mexicans exchanging their homeland for a life in the United States.[54] However for many Chicanos who were not the descendants of the first one-hundred thousand Mexicans that were gained through the Treaty of Guadalupe, the idea that the imaginary savior nation was wrong surprised them. In other words many Chicanos had an image of the United States as a great

---

[53] Ybarra, 178.

[54] Burton Kirkwood, *The History of Mexico* (Westport, CT: Greenwood Press, 2000), 175-177.

nation that supported freedom and democracy, but this image was shattered for Chicanos when the Vietnam War occurred. Many Mexican-American Vietnam War veterans were still patriotic but had grown suspicious and critical of the American government. Thus, their identity was altered into being a more cautious patriotic one.

The patriotism that Chicano soldiers had before the Vietnam War and in the early phases of the war was attached with family and with religion. No matter how controversial the conflict in Vietnam was one of its primary purposes was to end the spread of communism, and Lyndon Johnson believed that by defeating communists in Vietnam somehow that would ensure that communism did not present itself into the United States. Mexican-Americans had a natural inclination against communism. The rhetoric of Vladimir Lenin and his hostility towards religion did not capture the positive political sentiments of Chicanos.

Roman Catholicism in the Chicano and Mexican culture has become a symbol of hope, faith, and mestizaje. In December of 1531 the Virgin of Guadalupe appeared to an Indigenous peasant named Juan Diego near the mountains of Mexico City. The Virgin of Guadalupe appeared to him with brown skin like the skin of the Indigenous and spoke to Juan Diego in Nahuatl the language of many Indigenous people of Mexico. She ordered him to build him a church at the site of Tepeyac, and gave him Castillian roses which do not grow in December to prove that she had truly appeared.[55] The Virgin of Guadalupe came to symbolize mestizaje in the manner that she was a symbol to the Spanish and the Indigenous that she was worthy and needed to be respected. The color of her skin was an indicator to the Spanish that she stood on the behalf of the Indigenous people of Mexico, and that she demanded there to be peace among the Spanish and the Indigenous. As time progressed Roman Catholicism was spread throughout all of New Spain through the establishment of missions. The Spanish and the Indigenous mixed heavily with each other and produced mestizos or people of European and Native American descent. Chicanos who desired to stay close to their culture tried not to let go of Roman Catholicism and to the Virgin

---

[55] John Mini, *The Aztec Virgin: The Secret Mystical Tradition of Our Lady of Guadalupe* (Sausalito, CA: Trans-Hyperborean Institute of Science, 2000), 40-49.

of Guadalupe, because they provide a basis for morality and beliefs.

Communism on the other hand has a variety of notions within its doctrine that outline compassion for other human-beings and calls for a just society, but it calls for a suppression of religion. The problem with Christianity is that in the tenets of true Christianity pacificism is expected of a true Christian. Pacificism does not win a proletarian revolution. According to many communists only brute force can conquer capitalism, and that is one reason why communism stands against religion.[56] Karl Marx viewed religion as a tool that was created by the wealthy in order to create a sense of false hope for the working classes in order to keep them docile. Lenin was particularly hostile towards religion and identified atheism as an inseparable part of scientific socialism. He stated that religion must be combatted, and that religion was a reactionary method by the bourgeoisie to enslave the masses.[57]

---

[56] Leslie Mason, "The Conflict Between Communism and Religion," *The Communist Review* (2007), http://www.marxists.org/history/international/comintern/sections/br itain/periodicals/communist_review/1924/02/mason.htm (accessed January 3, 2013).

[57] Vladimir Ilich Lenin, *Essay on Religion by Lenin*, (Forgotten

To the Chicano communism stood against his beliefs, faith, and culture. In the early stages of the Vietnam War Chicanos sympathized with what was occurring in Vietnam. Many saw the fight against North Vietnam and the communists as a noble act, and wanted to see democracy established in South Vietnam. In the early years of America's involvement in the war Vietnamese Catholics from North Vietnam fled by the hundreds of thousands to South Vietnam in the effort to escape religious persecution by Ho Chi Minh and the communists. Ngo Dinh Diem the ruler of South Vietnam along with the United States saw this as an opportunity to rally support for democracy and the freedom of religious expression in South Vietnam. Strong efforts were made by the Roman Catholic Church to let the world know what was occurring in Vietnam by sending popular religious clergymen and women to Vietnam. The priest Patrick O'Connor chronicled the sufferings of the refugees and Pope Pius XII showed strong support for South Vietnam.[58]

Even though many Chicanos heavily sympathized with Vietnamese Catholics and stood against communism

Books, 2012), 10.

[58] Jacobs, 136-137.

they lost the belief that they were fighting communism in Vietnam. Juan Ramirez asserts that he felt that he was not acting as a true Catholic when he was relocating villagers during Johnson's Strategic Hamlet Program. Ramirez describes feeling nothing like he thought he would feel during war. The test of manhood was not there, and he remembered that it was nothing like the army conquests of his childhood hero John Wayne.[59] Killing people became a contradiction for Chicano soldiers that many of them struggled with.

The act of being a warrior had been a cultural characteristic for Mexican-Americans for centuries but killing people was a contradiction to their religious identity. Mike Serrano recalled that he felt guilty and confused about being a soldier and taking part in killing enemy combatants. At one point in his tour of Vietnam he went to speak to a Catholic priest, and confronted him. Serrano asked the priest how the priest could give the soldiers blessings from God right before they went out into the jungle to kill people. Serrano confessed that the answer the priest referenced to from the Old Testament was not

---

[59] Ramirez, 42-43.

satisfactory to him, and that it did not change the guilt he felt from the violence he experienced.[60] From these accounts it can be inferred that war and brutality never bring about true peace or justice.

For several Chicano soldiers the war brought a confliction in the sense of their Catholic or Christian religious identity. Antonio P. Bustamante discussed his feelings of duality between right and wrong in an oral history. Bustamante declared that he had no regrets and yet at the same time some regrets regarding his participation in the war in Vietnam. He did not regret fighting communism, like many Chicanos he felt animosity and hostility toward communism. However he did feel a strong regret for participating in a war that cost the lives of more than 58,000 military servicemen and women. Bustamante reminisced with regret at the destruction of Vietnamese lives, children, property, and land by the military. He averred that as a Catholic these things that occurred in Vietnam have been difficult to cope with.[61]

---

[60] Dominguez, 129.

[61] Bustamante, Antonio P. 2010. Interview by Debbie Lopez. March 7. Transcript, Veterans History Project, The Library of Congress, Washington, DC.

The war in Vietnam changed the religious characteristic of identity in Chicanos by questioning how even in the fight against communism a religious institution could stand for war. The inhumanity that many Mexican-American veterans witnessed and experienced created a sense of confliction for many of them. The war allowed Chicanos to question certain notions of the Catholic Church and while it may not have created atheists out of Mexican-American veterans it did create awareness that the Church may not always be correct. Many Chicanos after their participation in the war seemed to veer more towards the writings of the Catholic monk Thomas Merton. Merton stood on the side of pacifism. He heavily criticized Karl Marx for his desire to spread atheism and to combat religion.[62] However Merton also criticized the use of violence to accomplish peace, justice, or democracy, and was a strong opponent to American foreign policy in Vietnam. To make war in Vietnam was not an act of God even if it was in the effort to fight communism.[63] For many

---

[62] Thomas Merton, *Conjectures of a Guilty Bystander* (Garden City, NY: Doubleday & Company, Inc., 1968), 21-23.

[63] Thomas Merton, "Note for Ave Maria," *Passion for Peace:*

Chicano veterans the war in Vietnam was not truly fighting communism it was instead defending American corporate interests and protecting an oppressive dictatorship; one that was initially headed by Ngo Dinh Diem and then replaced by another headed by Nguyen Van Thieu.

In the Vietnam War there existed a large force that drove Chicanos as well as other soldiers to experience changes in their identities and in their perspectives regarding the validity of the war. Ngo Dinh Diem and Nguyen Van Thieu became the two most powerful men in the Republic of South Vietnam. They came to ostensibly espouse democracy and a parliamentary system. However the reality was far from the idealism of democratic institutions, and in practice the people of South Vietnam perceived of Diem and Thieu's policies as authoritarian.

When Diem became president of South Vietnam he deterred the land redistributions that the Viet Cong had muscled through coercion. The Viet Cong had managed to intimidate landowners in South Vietnam to vacate their land and then the Viet Cong redistributed the land to peasant farmers. However landowners composed a large

The Social Essays, ed. William H. Shannon (New York, NY: The Crossroad Publishing Company, 1997) 323.

segment of Diem's political followers and many landowners were also Catholic, so Diem reversed the land seizures and returned the landowners their property. Diem's regime did not conduct these policies in a peaceful manner and was known to be quite barbaric in accomplishing his objectives.[64] Diem did not seek to share much of his powers either and became the antithesis of democracy as he sought to centralize power.[65] Democracy was not a virtue that Diem shared with America however American officials like Eisenhower, John Foster Dulles, Kennedy, and Johnson saw Diem as the man that could at least keep communism from taking over South Vietnam.

Mexican-American soldiers were not oblivious to the atrocities that occurred in South Vietnam, and saw the nation as essentially backwards. Ray a former sergeant in the Army described that he saw South Vietnam as a place that endorsed immoral behavior. Ray discussed Saigon as a place where prostitution flourished and drinking and drug-

---

[64] Michael H. Hunt, ed., *A Vietnam War Reader: A Documentary from American and Vietnamese Perspectives* (Chapel Hill, NC: The University of North Carolina Press, 2010), 44-45.

[65] Jacobs, 183.

use was prevalent.[66] Raul a former Army soldier also discussed his opinion of Saigon and the South Vietnamese government. Raul averred that he never questioned that communism was wrong, because of its animosity towards religion and its desire to simply concentrate power from capitalist moguls to communist moguls. However he questioned what was right about Thieu regime, because he saw that it neglected the people of South Vietnam. Raul described Saigon as the city of a million prostitutes and beggars, and questioned if that was what America was fighting to establish.[67] Perhaps what Chicanos saw in South Vietnamese cities like Saigon led them to believe that America was losing the war and not achieving a real objective.

Chicano soldiers experienced several defeats in morale in the war in Vietnam that affected their identity and changed how they felt towards the war. The largest collection of attacks by the communist forces that affected morale was the Tet Offensive spearheaded by the Viet

---

[66] Ybarra, 124.

[67] Ybarra, 66.

Cong or National Liberation Front. The plans for the *Tet Mau Than* or New Year of the Monkey offensive were completed in 1967 by North Vietnamese diplomats in Hanoi. The offensive was geared towards breaking the South Vietnamese armed forces and convincing Americans that the war was unwinnable by targeting urban areas in South Vietnam.[68]

The Tet Offensive began on January 31, 1968 with the communist forces numbering above 80,000. The Viet Cong and other guerillas attacked almost all provincial capitals and most major cities from the Demilitarized Zone to the Gulf of Thailand. However the most important battles took place in Saigon, Quang Tri, Tam Ky, Hue City, Khe Sanh, and Chu Lai.[69] The battles were fierce and claimed the lives of many soldiers and civilians. The Viet Cong massacred many South Vietnamese non-combatants which added to the shock that the Tet Offensive produced in American soldiers and South Vietnamese soldiers. The numbers are not certain but estimates state that after the

---

[68] James H. Willbanks, *The Tet Offensive: A Concise History* (New York, NY: Columbia University Press, 2007), 10-11.

[69] Willbanks, 30.

three phases of the Tet Offensive around 40,000 to 80,000 communist troops were killed while 14,000 civilians also lost their lives.[70]

In discussing military strategy the Tet Offensive was a complete failure for the communist forces. While they proved that they could launch an offensive of such a great size on the American and South Vietnamese militaries they took heavy casualties and lost many soldiers. However the Tet Offensive managed to crush the morale of soldiers and Chicano soldiers felt the pinch. Henry Hernandez who served in the Marines recalled that the fight for Hue City was gruesome and endless. The resistance that American forces encountered in taking control of Hue City was fierce. Hernandez stated that his Marines took heavy casualties and that the fight lasted twenty-one days in order to defeat the Viet Cong guerillas.[71] The shock tactic that the guerillas in the Tet Offensive employed also brought a heightened sense of awareness by soldiers. In other words troops in general felt less fearful of danger in the rear areas but after the Tet Offensive it was typical of soldiers to carry grenades and other weapons with them constantly in areas

[70] Ibid., 81.
[71] Dominguez, 32-33.

that were once considered safe.[72] Even though the American forces inflicted a much higher casualty rate on the communist forces during the Tet Offensive the Viet Cong and other guerillas had managed to distort the mentality of the Americans.

Mexican-American soldiers and civilians began to grow impatient with the effort to deter communism from spreading into South Vietnam and began to view the war as unwinnable. Many Chicanos at home became deeply involved in the anti-war movement as they saw the war becoming too large. By 1968 the Johnson administration had about 600,000 troops stationed in Vietnam.[73] Many of these troops were Chicanos because of the program that the Johnson administration had instituted seeking to draft young men from urban areas into the military in order to "improve" their futures. As a result of the Tet Offensive and Johnson's troop escalation in South Vietnam Chicanos at home expressed their staunch disapproval with the war and even took part in several moratoriums with the goal of

---

[72] Garcia.

[73] U.S. Department of Defense, *Melvin R. Laird*, Secretary of Defense Histories (Washington, DC, 2012).

ending the draft of Chicanos into the military.[74] While not all Chicanos agreed with staging protests to end the war in Vietnam, the morale of many Chicanos that fought in the war did decline.

The American support for the dictatorships and corrupt regimes of Diem and Thieu made Chicano soldiers feel that they were playing an oppressive role in the war instead of successfully deterring communism from spreading into South Vietnam. The goal of seeing a South Vietnamese government that truly tried to help its people, and was dedicated to democratic elections was not seen by Chicano troops. Therefore their morale and spirit of fighting the war decreased and changed their attitudes towards governments going to war. Their identities regarding war as a means of accomplishing change were affected by witnessing these dictatorships. The Tet Offensive simply managed to demonstrate to Chicano soldiers that the people of South Vietnam were not content with the status quo regime, and that American politicians were not doing what needed to be done to bring about true democracy in South Vietnam.

---

[74] Oropeza, 135.

The escalation of soldiers into Vietnam and the Tet Offensive were two notions that lowered morale for Mexican-American soldiers. However the issue of racism and racial tensions was also a factor in the diminishing support for the war among Chicano soldiers, and racism affected the identity of Chicanos after the war. Discrimination was not a new concept to Mexican-Americans during the war, but it was surprising to many as many Hispanics did not expect to feel discrimination in the military. It was hard to grasp the fact that Chicanos were in the military to fight for America, and that their sacrifice did not make them American enough.

Hispanics were subjected to racism before the war in Vietnam, and even segregation was not uncommon for them to experience. In the state of Texas the separation of Hispanics from other European-Americans became a social custom. When the Texas Revolution had succeeded in separating Texas from Mexico Hispanics were viewed as untrustworthy. Towns in Texas were usually separated into three parts which consisted of an Anglo section, a Hispanic section, and a Black section. Chicanos could not interact with Anglo-Americans in churches, restaurants, theatres, and many other public places. Schools were also segregated but because Hispanics were partially White and considered White by authorities Hispanic schools did not receive the funding of the separate but equal clause.[75] Chicanos had to endure segregation in the state of Texas until the Supreme Court ruled in *Hernández v. State of Texas* in 1954 that Jim Crow laws could not be applied to Hispanics.

The state of California did not offer any more equality than the state of Texas did. There existed strong prejudice against Chicanos in California, and school segregation was quite common. Laws were enacted in the late 1800s that prohibited Native-American, Black, and Asian children from attending school with Anglo-American children. Hispanic students were also discriminated against in California, and school segregation for Chicanos did not end until a federal appellate court upheld in *Mendez v. Westminster* in 1947 that Hispanics could not be discriminated against in public schools and that segregation of Hispanics was unconstitutional.[76] However the history of

[75] Texas State Historical Association, "Segregation," http://www.tshaonline.org/handbook/online/articles/pks01 (accessed January 20, 2013).

[76] National Archives, "School Desegregation and Civil Rights

segregation regarding Chicanos did not deter Hispanics from enlisting voluntarily into the military during the Vietnam War.

Many Mexican-Americans viewed the military as a means to gain full American acceptance. Chicanos come from a mixed heritage of European and Indigenous ancestry that is now living in the United States. The issues that they have had with racism and discrimination made them feel like they were second-class citizens unable to gain full citizenship or full acceptance into American society. Enlistments into the military and military service were ways that Mexican-Americans could be accepted by non-Hispanic Americans at least in theory.[77]

Chicano soldiers felt discrimination in the military and that changed their identity and how they viewed American society. Juan Ramirez discusses his encounters with racism and talks about his squad leader named Jensen. Jensen was racist and hated minorities. At the time that Ramirez met him Jensen did not have much time left in his

Stories: Orange County, California,"
http://www.archives.gov/philadelphia/education/desegregation/orange-county.html (accessed January 21, 2013).
[77] Oropeza, 43-44.

tour of duty, and because of his short time Jensen would send minorities into the most dangerous missions and areas.[78] Towards Jensen's last few weeks in Vietnam he would send Ramirez and his squad to patrol areas while he would stay at the command post. Ramirez discusses that he exploded with rage and told his commanding officer that Jensen was no longer fit for duty, and that Jensen did not care about minorities or their safety.[79] What Ramirez experienced with his racist squad leader in Vietnam was simply a representation of the discrimination that existed in America at the time, and that had travelled with his platoon to the war in Vietnam. Except that in this case racism became a problem in order to survive as Chicanos were constantly being put in positions of danger because they were considered less important and more expendable.

The notion of racism was something that plagued Chicano soldiers in many things that they did during the Vietnam War. The notion of being promoted to higher ranks in the military was more difficult for Chicano soldiers than it was for Anglo soldiers. Juan Jose Pena who

---

[78] Ramirez, 52.

[79] Ibid., 65.

would later become a doctor in Mexican-American Studies recalls his experiences with racism in the military as condescending. Pena remembers an occasion when his senior non-commissioned officer told him that he had great skills and discipline but that he would never become a commissioned officer.[80] Pena believed that the NCO was alluding to the fact that minorities made up a large segment of enlisted and drafted soldiers but made up a very small segment of college-educated officers.

Racism towards Chicanos during the Vietnam War era was also institutionalized by the federal government in a certain way. In other words Lyndon Johnson, Robert McNamara, and the military had instituted a program called Project 100,000 which sought to lower the standards of the Armed Forces qualification test and to provide remedial help for those who were unable to pass the tests.[81] What Project 100,000 really did was that it sought to recruit more Hispanics, Blacks, and Native-Americans who because of

---

[80] Dominguez, 165.

[81] The Vietnam Center and Archive, "Vietnam Archive Robert S. McNamara Resources," http://www.vietnam.ttu.edu/resources/mcnamara/ (accessed February 1, 2013).

inferior educational systems could not pass the qualification tests and were therefore unfit for military service. Draft deferments for college educated students proved that minorities were bigger targets for military service as many Chicanos note that it was almost impossible for them to obtain a draft deferment because of poor education. Louis Rodriguez a former soldier recalls that he was drafted into the Army and that he had no choice regarding which branch of the military he could serve in or where he could be stationed.[82] Rodriguez is just one of many Chicanos who were drafted into the military and for many reasons regarding socio-economic conditions, patriotism, or ideas to combat communism chose to stay and not try to dodge the draft. Racism however played a part in the amount of Chicanos who were drafted into the military during the Vietnam War at the federal level. The draft made Chicanos feel like they were second-class citizens in that they were not afforded the option of joining the military but were required to. This form of institutionalized discrimination further added to the

---

[82] Rodriguez, Louis. 2005. Interview by Debra Murphy. July 28. Transcript, Veterans History Project, The Library of Congress, Washington, DC.

alienation that Chicanos felt towards government. In other words the draft and Project 100,000 changed the political identity of Chicanos, and made them feel fear towards government.

When Chicano soldiers returned from the war in Vietnam discrimination towards them continued at various degrees. Juan Ramirez recalls being pulled over by a police officer who mocked his military service and accused Ramirez of being a bathroom cleaner in the military.[83] Chicanos also experienced difficulties in obtaining employment because of their ethnicity and prior military service. Joaquin M. Jauregui a former soldier in the Army claimed that he got fired from a job at a telephone company because he was not an American citizen even though he had served in the Vietnam War. Jauregui admitted that that incident drove him to consume alcohol in heavier amounts.[84] Racism was a factor that affected the identities of Chicano soldiers, and that Chicanos had to deal with. The incidents of discrimination that occurred in the Vietnam War were

---

[83] Ramirez, 91.

[84] Jauregui, Joaquin M. 2009. Interview by Efrain Avila. March 11. Transcript, Veterans History Project, The Library of Congress, Washington, DC.

representative of the problems that American society had at the time with prejudice against Hispanics.

All of the factors that changed the identity of Chicanos in the Vietnam War were exacerbated by the use of drugs and alcohol. Racism was a problem that Hispanics have had to deal with for all of their lives but the war was unique in that drugs and alcohol were used as a means of recreation by some soldiers during and after the conflict. The hippie movement in America and new ideas regarding peace and free love were entangled within heavy drug use. That culture of using drugs and alcohol to free the mind was brought to the Vietnam War by American soldiers. When soldiers returned to the United States many of them encountered a society in which the use of illegal substances was on the rise. As a result many Chicano veterans turned into drug-addicts and alcohol abusers.

The use of drugs and alcohol for many Chicano soldiers began in the jungles of Vietnam. Southeast Asia has been a producer of heroin and opium for centuries, and as Juan Ramirez described it heroin and marijuana could be found in abundance in Vietnam at very cheap prices.[85]

---

[85] Ramirez, 112-113.

Using drugs and alcohol became a form of escape for many soldiers who were in Vietnam and who did not want to be there. Chicanos who were constantly facing death in the front lines of South Vietnam numbed the mental pain by taking drugs and alcohol. Officers would turn a blind eye to the use of alcohol by the "juicers" and to the use of drugs by the "slammers."

For many Chicanos the use of drugs and alcohol may have had to do with the fact that many of them came from impoverished backgrounds and poor neighborhoods where drugs were already a problem. Since draft deferments were typically unavailable to minorities and Project 100,000 made sure to enlist young people from poorer urban neighborhoods it cannot be surprising that drug culture was exported to Vietnam. The anti-war movement and the hippie movement also made sure to incorporate middle class young adults into drug culture. Soldiers began using marijuana as early as 1963 when the war was still in its early stages, and in 1967 a federal investigation revealed that marijuana was used at least sixteen times at the Marine Corps brig in Da Nang. Heroin was used by an estimated 15 to 20 percent of soldiers in the

Mekong Delta, and could cost as low as $1 dollar per dose.[86] Not all Chicano soldiers were drug users but there was a significant amount of soldiers from all backgrounds that became heavier drug users and alcohol consumers because of the Vietnam War.

When many Mexican-American soldiers returned home from Vietnam the addiction to drugs and alcohol continued. In 1973 a White House coordinated survey discovered that out of the thousands of heroin users that returned from the war in Vietnam one-third were still addicted.[87] The combination of depression from the atrocities that many Chicano veterans had experienced in the war as well as the helplessness that many felt upon their return home fueled the increasing turn to self-medication. This self-medication came in the form of using substances that were readily available without the need to seek medical help or a prescription. The trauma that they suffered in the jungles of Vietnam was brought home and was exacerbated

---

[86] Peter Brush, "Higher and Higher: American Drug Use in Vietnam," *Vietnam*, December 2002, http://www.library.vanderbilt.edu/central/Brush/American-drug-use-vietnam.htm (accessed February 3, 2013).

[87] Ibid.

by problems that included racism, unemployment, and the neglect of society towards the Vietnam veteran.

The feelings of guilt and remorse regarding the problems associated with the war in Vietnam were one of the causes for increased alcohol and drug abuse by Chicano veterans. David a former Corporal in the Army described his feelings of remorse by stating that he felt that there were things that he could not change. People that he had to kill in the war brought back bad memories and nightmares. For a long time David drank alcohol in dangerous amounts in order to avoid the nightmares in which the Vietnam War would all come back. He confessed that he was able to escape these dreams because he was constantly inebriated. [88] The desire to escape the memories of the war became a common goal for many Hispanic soldiers who felt anxiety about the destruction the war had caused.

Drugs and alcohol became a prolonged problem for many Hispanic veterans who could not break away from the perils of addiction. Abran F. Montoya a former soldier admits that one thing that the Vietnam War left within him were issues of addiction. Montoya averred that after the

---

[88] Ybarra, 144-145.

war his consumption of alcohol increased in order to cope with the changes from being in a war zone to being in a more calm area. He would constantly have flashbacks and nightmares and he admits that his problem with alcohol affected his marriage. However he declares that it was the love and compassion of his wife that helped him become stronger and quit drinking.[89] The neglect that many Chicanos encountered by the federal government upon their return from the war created resentment among veterans. For many years after the war veterans were ignored by the government and there were not enough services that targeted the problems that veterans and Chicano veterans especially were going through.

The use of drugs and alcohol by soldiers upon their return from Vietnam changed their identity as many were no longer the people that they used to be. Louis Rodriguez declares that he became a hard-core alcoholic, and that when he was intoxicated he would argue with his wife. However she also pushed him to seek help even though it proved to be a tough journey to recovery for him.[90] Juan

---

[89] Montoya, Abran F., Jr. 2002. Interview by Dena R. Montoya Osborn. December 7. Transcript, Veterans History Project, The Library of Congress, Washington, DC.

Ramirez in his book describes the issues he had with drugs and alcohol upon his return from the war as detrimental to his family. Ramirez however would take years to recover from his problems with drugs and alcohol and ended up divorced from his first wife due to his problems coping with a non-combative environment.[91] The alcohol and drug abuse problems that many Chicano soldiers experienced in the Vietnam War and upon their return to America managed to destroy families and change who these Chicanos were. For many who were lucky sobriety came as a blessing but for a few others homelessness and death took a toll on their lives.

American society helped to create a negative atmosphere for Chicano veterans upon their return home. Antonio P. Bustamante described his return to America as hostile, because protesters and hippies treated them with disdain. Bustamante declares that upon landing at the airport protesters demonstrated animosity towards him and other veterans by insulting them and throwing things at

---

[90] Rodriguez.

[91] Ramirez, 160-161.

them. He notes that even his family and friends were not as compassionate with him as they should have been.[92] It was hypocritical of Americans to treat veterans in this manner, because veterans especially Hispanics had little choice in going off to fight the war in Vietnam. Many Chicanos came from impoverished backgrounds in which there were few opportunities for a better future, and college draft deferments were almost completely out of the question. McNamara's Project 100,000 made minorities an even greater target for the draft, and fleeing to another country was not a part and did not appeal to Mexican-American cultural dynamics.

Racism influenced how Chicano Vietnam veterans felt about their identity of being Americans and Mexicans synchronously. The Chicano veteran had to cope with the idea that he had served in an unpopular war and that he was poorly welcomed home. Even though he had left his country for patriotism or simply because he had no other option he was not received as a better American for participating in the conflict. Upon the return to America

---

[92] Bustamante.

many Chicanos were still treated as second-class citizens not just by their government but also by other Americans.

The violence and brutality that many Chicano veterans experienced in Vietnam created severe changes in many of them that influenced their characters, personalities, and emotions. The medical term for this disorder that was brought back to America by veterans was titled Post-Traumatic Stress Disorder (PTSD), and its symptoms included upsetting memories, nightmares, flashbacks, feelings of hopelessness, and survivors' guilt among many more. PTSD affected veterans and their families and was a disorder in which the government did not rapidly create programs to provide medical treatment for it or its side effects. Chicano veterans had a lot of problems associated with PTSD due to discrimination in VA hospitals and the strong feelings of denial regarding symptoms of the disorder.[93]

In the dialogue regarding PTSD many Hispanic soldiers felt that the federal government as well as American society had neglected their problems, and in

---

[93] Sonya Rhee and Charley Trujillo, *Discussion Guide: Soldados Chicanos in Viet Nam* (Arlington, VA: Public Broadcasting Service, 2003), 4-5.

some instances ridiculed their service in Vietnam. Bobby J. Montano a former Hispanic soldier reported that he struggled with his problems of PTSD for a long time, and that he felt that the government did not try to tackle the issues of PTSD as much as they could have. Montano instead of seeking help from a federal program to battle his PTSD symptoms eventually joined a support group which was started up by other Vietnam veterans. He stated that relationships with other people were difficult for him because of his problems associated with PTSD.[94] Relationships with family and close friends were deeply affected by PTSD in Chicano soldiers who had returned from Vietnam. Juan Ramirez describes his problems with the disorder as shattering to his relationship with his wife. Ramirez recalled one incident in which he had a flashback of the war and had ran to the edge of a cliff. His wife chased him down and he realized that he had problems due to the war and that he needed to seek help.[95]

---

[94] Montano, Bobby J. 2011. Interview by Rachel Trujillo. October 26. Transcript, Veterans History Project, The Library of Congress, Washington, DC.

[95] Ramirez, 160-161.

The problem with PTSD for many Chicanos was that their culture of machismo was too strong to recognize that they were mentally helpless. Older generations of Chicano veterans who had fought in Korea and in both World Wars had suppressed symptoms of PTSD and covered them with machismo and alcohol use. However the war in Vietnam was different for Chicanos because they did not receive the treatment that many older veterans received. In other words when Chicanos returned home they returned to a society that looked down upon Vietnam veterans while veterans from World War I and World War II still experienced racism but returned to a society where their service was somewhat appreciated. Joaquin M. Jauregui demonstrates his resentment towards a society that was not the victims of the draft or who had the means to avoid the draft by recalling that when someone discovered that he was a veteran of Vietnam they automatically assumed things about him. Jauregui averred that he could never wear his uniform in the United States without someone acting in a hostile manner towards him.[96]

---

[96] Jauregui.

The mental problems that were associated with PTSD affected Chicano veterans in a negative manner, and contributed to their problems in finding and holding employment. PTSD hurt Chicanos who could have been productive members of society, who instead abused drugs and alcohol as a means of self-medication. Without the strong support of government agencies to provide outreach programs for veterans of color Chicanos with PTSD resorted to find solutions of their own sometimes productive but many times destructive. As a result homelessness in the United States rose especially in the veteran category. The National Coalition for Homeless Veterans concluded that 23 percent of all homeless people in America are veterans, and that of these 47 percent are Vietnam veterans.[97]

PTSD was a major result for veterans of the Vietnam War and so was the physical ailments that resulted from the military's use of a defoliant known as Agent Orange. The military would use the chemical that contained dioxin in order to destroy vegetation in the dense jungles of Vietnam. The purpose was to remove any cover which

---

[97] Rhee and Trujillo, 7.

would be of use to the communist forces; however dioxin has been proven to be highly toxic to humans. Numerous cancers and even heart disease have been attributed to Agent Orange, and these include cancer of the prostate, lymph nodes, spleen, liver, bone marrow, and many more.[98] It can be argued that the production of Agent Orange by the Monsanto Corporation and the Dow Chemical company was a way in which functionaries of the federal government profited from the war in Vietnam by handing down government contracts. The cost was high in the veteran community and proved to have severe physical ramifications for Chicano veterans.

Abran F. Montoya describes his problems with Agent Orange as detrimental to his health and to the relationship he has had with his family. Montoya's testimony confirms that the government was slow in their response to the issues associated with Agent Orange, and that at many points they neglected the repercussions. Montoya states that his diabetes, kidney problems, and blood problems have all been linked to his exposure to Agent Orange.[99] Ray a former Sergeant in the Army also

---

[98] US Department of Veterans Affairs, *Veterans' Diseases Associated With Agent Orange* (Washington, DC, 2012).

had severe problems linked to both PTSD and Agent Orange. He recalled that the military would release thousands of pounds of dioxin from helicopters and airplanes in order to defoliate the jungle. However he remembers that the soldiers were told that it was harmless to humans, and that sometimes they were misled regarding its use. Sometimes they were misinformed that Agent Orange was really mosquito repellant. Ray's experience with the side effects of Agent Orange was terrifying to him and his family. He had trouble talking to his wife and family about his experiences in Vietnam and about the physical side effects that were happening to him. He remembers that his body would constantly break-out in rashes that were unexplainable by doctors and that at the same time he would have nightmares about the war as a symptom of PTSD.[100]

The difficulties that Chicano veterans of the Vietnam War experienced with PTSD and Agent Orange changed their physical identities. Repercussions came for Chicanos as many of these veterans were neglected by the federal government and treated as expendable in the

[99] Montoya.
[100] Ybarra, 126-127.

military. Their mental and physical identities of who they once were for many Chicanos dramatically altered after their participation in the war. The tension and hostility that many Hispanics feel towards government can be interpreted as a reaction to the neglect that the military and government agencies demonstrated towards these issues. The problems that were created between Chicano veterans and their families were in fact changes in cultural norms in Mexican-American culture. Communication between a veteran and his family deteriorated in the face of the struggle against the symptoms of PTSD and Agent Orange. The pride that many Chicanos thought they would feel due to their participation in the war for many of them did not exist.

The Vietnam War for many Chicanos had several changes in how they felt about being Mexican-American. The war changed many parts of their identity that built who they are. The characteristics of their identity were altered by the war, and almost all the factors that construct a human being's identity were changed. Chicano soldiers experienced changes in the way that they relate to family members and friends. The cultural tie that Hispanics share in being emotionally close to family was distorted by their participation in the war, and this led Chicanos to be more withdrawn from family and friends. The cultural tradition that Mexicans and Mexican-Americans had established as a means to survive amid poverty and struggles with oppressive governments was rattled by the emotional problems that the Vietnam War caused. This was quite possibly due to the violence against civilians that Chicano soldiers encountered and may have been a part of. This was also due to the brutal tactics that the communist forces used against American soldiers and civilians that caused many soldiers to return from Vietnam traumatized.

The perception of religion and patriotism was another characteristic of the identity of Chicanos that was altered by the Vietnam conflict. As several Chicano soldiers encountered a condoning voice in the Catholic perspective regarding the war against communism in Vietnam, many questioned this controversial notion. Many Mexican-Americans stood firmly against the anti-religious tenets of communism, but many understood Christianity's stance against killing people as well. This caused a confliction to occur in the way that Chicanos viewed the war as a necessary evil in order to fight communism. It was not clear to some Chicano soldiers how a religious institution could preach tolerance, love, and mercy and yet synchronously condone killing people in Vietnam. As a result some of these soldiers remained Catholics but became suspicious of the leadership of the Church while others became withdrawn from religion altogether. The infallibility of the Catholic Church came into question and was doubted by many soldiers.

Patriotism was a factor that was altered by the Mexican-American participation in the war as well. The Chicano mestizo who comes from a background of Indigenous descent which can have roots in tribes such as the Comanche, Apache, Yaqui, Tarascan, Aztec, and many more Indigenous tribes of Mexico and the Southwestern United States has been able to feel a strong connection to the lands of the Southwest. For a Chicano the feeling of being from the continents of the Americas goes back thousands of years when the first Native Americans crossed the Bering land-bridge and eventually settled in the various parts of the Americas. Many Chicanos have accepted that they are Indigenous, Spanish, Mexican, and American and that they celebrate various parts of all four cultures. Antonio P. Bustamante stated that the one thing that he wanted society to remember about his participation in the Vietnam War was that he was proud of being an American of Mexican and Indigenous descent.[101] Bustamante is not alone in his feelings of patriotism towards being a mestizo, many Chicano veterans still feel proud of being Mexican-American mestizos. The Vietnam War did not take away Chicanos' patriotism; instead it instilled a fear towards government, and a withdrawal from following government actions without second thoughts. In other words many Chicanos were still very proud to be Mexican-Americans but many became skeptical of government.

The support the federal government gave to the dictatorships of Ngo Dinh Diem and Nguyen Van Thieu was a reason why this skepticism towards government grew among Chicano Vietnam veterans. The perception of government in the identity of Chicanos was altered because of the validity of the war in Vietnam. Mexican-Americans have long had doubts about the actions of government due to the land incursions of the Manifest Destiny policies of

---

[101] Bustamante.

the federal government. Due to patriotism, a warrior culture, and the Chicano stance against communism many Mexican-Americans decided to serve in the war. However as the war's duration prolonged many soldiers observed that democracy was not being instituted in South Vietnam, and that oppressive dictatorships were being backed instead. The endorsing of corrupt governments in Vietnam helped to break the belief in positive government actions, and led Chicano veterans to become withdrawn from government. Many Chicano Vietnam veterans became discontent with protesters in America who blamed the soldiers for the actions of the war. The anger stems from the fact that many Chicanos did not have the resources to flee from the draft and had no choice but to serve in the military. Ralph Garcia stated that they claimed to be angry at government foreign policy but that in the end it would be lower echelon soldiers who would take the heat for what happened in Vietnam.[102]

The problem with discrimination that Chicanos experienced during the conflict in Vietnam was another factor that changed the identity of Chicano veterans.

---

[102] Garcia.

Prejudice against the ethnicity of Hispanics has always been an issue in the United States. Chicanos have joined the military as a way of becoming accepted as first-class citizens in a society that deems the Hispanic culture as inferior and second-rate to Anglo culture. Racism has not been able to conquer the Chicano mind, and Chicanos have risen up to the challenge of discrimination. Discrimination in military branches has just been an extension of the institutionalized discrimination that Hispanics have suffered in American society. When Chicanos returned home their struggle against prejudice continued as many found it difficult to find gainful employment or obtaining educational benefits.

The atrocities that many Chicano soldiers were exposed to in the Vietnam War resulted in changes in their physical and mental health or in the characteristics of their identity. PTSD became a problem that affected how Chicanos held relationships with family members, friends, and people of the outside world. Chicano veterans had difficulties communicating with their loved ones and for many the result was self-medication in the form of alcohol and drug abuse. For many Chicanos divorce became common and for those who experienced severe symptoms of PTSD homelessness became common. The physically damaging effects of Agent Orange became another struggle that Vietnam veterans experienced. Dioxin produced a malevolent change in the physical attributes of many Mexican-American veterans that increased the social problems that they had.

The war in Vietnam was a war that produced changes in the identity of the more than 170,000 Mexican Americans who participated in it. The characteristics that comprise Mexican-American culture were altered by a government that sought to fix the world while it ignored its own social problems at home. The fight against communism and the details of the domino theory were not well thought out, and democracy in South Vietnam was never truly instituted. As a result many lives were lost in a war in which minorities were drafted and sent to the front lines to fight in disproportionate numbers. The negligence of the discrimination problems in the United States resulted in another front for Chicano veterans to deal with. They have continuously had to struggle with a society that denigrates Vietnam veterans and discriminates against

Chicanos, and they have had to fight for common civil rights against a government that institutionalized racism. The sacrifices that Chicanos made during the Vietnam War should not be forgotten or dismissed as irrelevant.

References

Brush, Peter. "Higher and Higher: American Drug Use in Vietnam."*Vietnam*, December 2002, http://www.library.vanderbilt.edu/central/Brush/American-drug-use-vietnam.htm (accessed February 3, 2013).

Bustamante, Antonio P. 2010. Interview by Debbie Lopez. March 7. Transcript, Veterans History Project, The Library of Congress, Washington, DC.

Cisneros, Sandra. *Woman Hollering Creek and Other Stories*. New York, NY: Vintage/Random House, 1992.

Dominguez, Gil. *They Answered the Call: Latinos in the Vietnam War*. Baltimore, MD: Publish America, 2004.

García, Mario T., and Sal Castro, *Blowout! Sal Castro & the Chicano Struggle for Educational Justice*. Chapel Hill, NC: The University of North Carolina Press, 2011.

Garcia, Ralph. 2002. Interview by Philip Shaull. December 17. Transcript, Veterans History Project, The Library of Congress, Washington, DC.

Hunt, Michael H., ed. *A Vietnam War Reader: A Documentary from American and Vietnamese Perspectives*. Chapel Hill, NC: The University of North Carolina Press, 2010.

Huntington, Samuel P. "The Hispanic Challenge." *Foreign Policy* no. 141 (March-April 2004): 30-45.

Jacobs, Seth. *America's Miracle Man in Vietnam: Ngo Dinh Diem, Religion, Race, and U.S. Intervention in Southeast Asia, 1950-1957*. Durham, NC: Duke University Press, 2004.

Jauregui, Joaquin M. 2009. Interview by Efrain Avila. March 11. Transcript, Veterans History Project, The Library of Congress, Washington, DC.

Kirkwood, Burton. *The History of Mexico*. Westport, CT: Greenwood Press, 2000.

Lenin, Vladimir Ilich. *Essay on Religion by Lenin.* Forgotten Books, 2012.

Lopez, Luis Muñiz. 2009. Interview by William L.
    Browne. August 7. Transcript, Veterans History
    Project, The Library of Congress, Washington, DC.

Mason, Leslie. "The Conflict Between Communism and
    Religion." *The Communist Review* (2007),
    http://www.marxists.org/history/international/comin
    tern/sections/britain/periodicals/communist_review/
    1924/02/mason.htm (accessed January 3, 2013).

Merton, Thomas. *Conjectures of a Guilty Bystander*.
    Garden City, NY: Doubleday & Company, Inc.,
    1968.

---. "Note for Ave Maria," *Passion for Peace: The Social
    Essays*, ed. William H. Shannon. New York, NY:
    The Crossroad Publishing Company, 1997.

Mini, John. *The Aztec Virgin: The Secret Mystical
    Tradition of Our Lady of Guadalupe*. Sausalito, CA:
    Trans-Hyperborean Institute of Science, 2000.

Montano, Bobby J. 2011. Interview by Rachel Trujillo. October 26. Transcript, Veterans History Project, The Library of Congress, Washington, DC.

Montoya, Abran F., Jr. 2002. Interview by Dena R. Montoya Osborn. December 7. Transcript, Veterans History Project, The Library of Congress, Washington, DC.

National Archives. "School Desegregation and Civil Rights Stories: Orange County, California." http://www.archives.gov/philadelphia/education/des egregation/orange-county.html (accessed January 21, 2013).

Nelson, Michael ed. *The Evolving Presidency: Addresses, Cases, Essays, Letters, Reports, Resolutions, Transcripts, and Other Landmark Documents, 1787-1998*. Washington, DC: Congressional Quarterly Inc., 1999.

Oropeza, Lorena. *¡Raza Si! ¡Guerra No! Chicano Protest and Patriotism During the Viet Nam War Era.* Berkeley, CA: University of California Press, 2005.

Ramirez, Juan. *A Patriot After All: the Story of a Chicano Vietnam Vet.* Albuquerque, NM: University of New Mexico Press, 1999.

Rhee, Sonya and Charley Trujillo. *Discussion Guide: Soldados Chicanos in Viet Nam.* Arlington, VA: Public Broadcasting Service, 2003.

Rodriguez, Louis. 2005. Interview by Debra Murphy. July 28. Transcript, Veterans History Project, The Library of Congress, Washington, DC.

Texas State Historical Association. "Segregation." http://www.tshaonline.org/handbook/online/articles/pks01 (accessed January 20, 2013).

The Vietnam Center and Archive. "Vietnam Archive Robert S. McNamara Resources."

http://www.vietnam.ttu.edu/resources/mcnamara/
(accessed February 1, 2013).

Trujillo, Charley. *Soldados: Chicanos in Viet Nam*. San
    Jose, CA: Chusma House Publications, 1990.

U.S. Department of Defense. *Melvin R. Laird*, Secretary of
    Defense Histories. Washington, DC, 2012.

U.S.Department of Veterans Affairs. *Veterans' Diseases
    Associated With Agent Orange*. Washington, DC,
    2012.

Willbanks, James H. *The Tet Offensive: A Concise History*.
    New York, NY: Columbia University Press, 2007.

Ybarra, Lea. *Vietnam Veteranos: Chicanos Recall the War*.
    Austin, TX: University of Texas Press, 2004.

CHAPTER THREE
THE SILVER SCREEN:
Chicano Vietnam Veterans in Film

The Vietnam War brought revenues to many industries that were involved in equipping troops with the weapons and munitions that were needed to fight the conflict against the communist forces. Companies such as Monsanto and DuPont made millions of dollars from the production of Agent Orange that was used to defoliate vegetation in Vietnam. The repercussions of the use of dioxin brought devastating effects on the Vietnamese people and on American soldiers who were exposed to the harmful chemicals that were used by military troops. Weapons manufacturers also made vast sums of money from the production of these tools of destruction. After the war however another industry made millions of dollars from producing works that used the Vietnam War as a popular theme, and that was the film industry. This chapter seeks to discuss how Mexican-Americans have been portrayed in popular Hollywood films about the Vietnam War.

One of the most popular films that was produced in the United States about the war in Vietnam was Oliver Stone's 1986 *Platoon*. The film *Platoon* sought to discuss themes that were not discussed in preceding films regarding the Vietnam War such as the 1968 film *The Green Berets*. Stone's film did succeed in venturing out into ideological areas that needed to be dissected. The film revolves around Chris Taylor whose a college dropout willing to join the military because he saw that it was an injustice for the working classes to fight a war that the wealthy chose to wage.[103]

Unlike *The Green Berets* which glorifies and romanticizes the Vietnam War, Stone's film discusses issues such as fragging and war crimes through the eyes of Taylor. In one scene Taylor finds a group of soldiers attempting to rape a couple of Vietnamese village girls so he challenges the soldiers to a fight which his Sergeant has to break up. That was a successful attempt by Stone to depict some of the things that occurred in the jungles of Vietnam that were not discussed or were ignored by films whose subject matter was the war in Vietnam. One of the

---

[103] Oliver Stone, *Platoon*, DVD, Hemdale Film Corporation and Orion Pictures, 1986.

main plot lines of the film *Platoon* was the animosity that two of Taylor's sergeants had for each other. Staff Sergeant Barnes played by Tom Berenger and Sergeant Elias played by Willem Dafoe despise one another and come to signify a good soldier versus a bad soldier binary. Sergeant Elias demands that Staff Sergeant Barnes be court-martialed for an illegal killing of a Vietnamese villager; however Staff Sergeant Barnes eventually creates a rouse in order to kill Sergeant Elias and therefore eliminate the threat of his testimony.[104] This plot line in Stone's film seeks to bring to the forefront the issue with fragging that soldiers in the Vietnam War experienced. It was also a binary of one soldier who believed that a war could be fought and won by respecting non-combatants and their property and of another soldier who represented the evils of war.

Stone's film *Platoon* underplays the role of Chicano soldiers in the Vietnam War even though at the same time it happens to be one of the only films that has Chicano soldiers in it. Hollywood has an issue with placing Hispanic actors in protagonist roles. Historically Hispanic actors seem to play roles in which they are the "foreign other,"

---

[104] Ibid.

what this comes to signify is that Hispanic-Americans are not portrayed as belonging to American society nor to mainstream American culture. Even when a Chicano or a Hispanic actor was born in the United States and speaks English in the same way that an Anglo-Saxon American speaks it he is still given acting roles in which he must speak with an accent or portray a foreigner. Hispanics have always comprised a notable proportion of America's population but they have been the most under-represented group of people in Hollywood films, and this remains unchanged even today.

It seems that Oliver Stone was aware of this fact when he wrote and directed *Platoon*, and so he did decide to incorporate Hispanics and Chicanos in his film. In his film there were three Hispanic characters; Francesco Quinn played Rhah, Paul Sanchez played Doc, and Chris Castillejo played Rodriguez.[105] Of the 31 soldiers in Taylor's platoon three of them were Hispanic or 9.6 percent of the platoon. Compared to other Vietnam War films this was actually quite the realization, but it still fell short of the true demographics of a random US Army combat platoon

---

[105] Ibid.

in Vietnam. It is a fact that Hispanics and Chicanos served in the Vietnam War in disproportionate numbers compared to the actual percentage of the population of Hispanics living in the United States. Given that Taylor's platoon was created at random at least 20 percent of the platoon should have represented Hispanics and Chicanos in the attempt to be fair and real to the war's demographics.

Another issue that Stone's film had in its portrayal of Hispanic and Chicano soldiers was their lack of depth. The character Taylor never took the time to explore where his Hispanic comrades were from or what they thought of the war. Most of the Hispanic and Chicano soldiers in the film would say one sentence during the film's entirety at most. This demonstrates that these soldiers were present only as background props, and that Stone never intended to discuss any of the issues that affected Hispanic soldiers in the Vietnam War. The character Taylor who came from an upper middle class family had no intention of learning about the problems that working class minorities had. Without the Hispanic soldiers having dialogue or a noteworthy script it is impossible to give this group of characters the depth that they deserved.

Another film in which Chicanos were portrayed as participating in the Vietnam War was Stanley Kubrick's 1987 film *Full Metal Jacket*. Kubrick also explored issues regarding the Vietnam War that were not popular to discuss such as war crimes and the military's poor screening of potential recruits.[106] This film revolves around the experiences of a soldier nicknamed Joker played by Matthew Modine. Joker enlists into the Marine Corps and completes his basic training in Parris Island, SC before being sent to Vietnam as a combat reporter. When he is in basic training a fellow recruit named Leonard Lawrence and nicknamed Gomer Pyle is bullied by other recruits and by the senior drill instructor Gunnery Sergeant Hartman played by R. Lee Ermy. Recruit Lawrence is slower than all the other recruits in the platoon, and it is inferred that he may be mentally unfit for duty in the Marine Corps. However Gunnery Sergeant Hartman pushes him to be a good Marine and this drives Recruit Lawrence to kill Hartman with his rifle and then to consequently commit suicide himself.[107] It is in this plot line that Kubrick is

---

[106] Stanley Kubrick, *Full Metal Jacket*, DVD, Harrier Films and Warner Bros. Pictures, 1987.

expressing the lowered standards that the military implemented during Vietnam. Kubrick is saying that Recruit Lawrence should have never been accepted into the military in the first place. In comparison with other films that discuss the Vietnam War Kubrick is one of the first directors to explore this phenomenon.

When Joker finds himself in Vietnam he and his friend Private First Class Rafter Man are sent on a mission to join a combat unit and write a report on their patrols. When they rendezvous with the combat platoon they speak to a soldier who is sitting beside a dead Viet Cong soldier who uses the dead soldier as a prop.[108] It can be inferred that Kubrick's intention was to express the de-humanization that the Vietnam War caused within the soldiers who served in the war. This was an example of the many different types of war crimes that occurred in this particular kind of war. In another scene of the film an ARVN soldier brings the platoon a prostitute and offers her to them for money.[109] This was clearly an allusion to the

---

[107] Ibid.

[108] Ibid.

[109] Ibid.

copious amounts of prostitutes that existed in South Vietnam at the time; however Kubrick did not directly give his opinion of these war crimes instead he would demonstrate the issue and let the viewer decide its morality.

The film did a poor job in its portrayal of Hispanic participation in the Vietnam War. In the entire film there was only one Hispanic soldier that Joker encountered named The Rock played by Sal Lopez.[110] The Rock's participation in the film was brief even though he did come to symbolize Hispanic participation in the Battle of Hue City. As with Oliver Stone's film *Platoon* the Chicano character lacked depth, his conversations were short, and the minutes he was shown on film were very meager.

The concept of the Chicano or Hispanic being almost absent in Vietnam War films can be seen in the films *Platoon* and *Full Metal Jacket*. However the concept of being completely absent from the silver screen can be seen in almost every other Hollywood film that uses the Vietnam War as its subject matter. The film *The Green Berets* is a prime example of a film that made sure to exclude Hispanic soldiers from the scenes of Vietnam.[111]

---

[110] Ibid.

This John Wayne film was produced as a propaganda piece with partial federal funding in order to gain support for the war effort. However it did not present the high number of minorities that were being drafted and who volunteered into combat. Worse than *The Green Berets* was the 1987 film *Hamburger Hill* which also felt that it did not need to use any Hispanics in the Battle for Hill 937 in the A Shau Valley.[112] The reality was that in the Battle for Hill 937 many Chicanos and other Hispanics fought as hard as any other American soldier. Paul Garcia Jr. was one of many Chicanos stationed in the Quang Tri Province and he made sergeant while he was in combat. When he was serving in Vietnam he said that he saw so much combat that he never had time to do anything else.[113] However the sacrifices that minorities made in every war that America has ever fought have gone almost completely ignored by Hollywood films.

---

[111] John Wayne, Ray Kellogg, and Mervyn LeRoy, *The Green Berets*, DVD, Warner Bros. and Seven Arts, 1968.

[112] John Irvin, *Hamburger Hill*, DVD, RKO Pictures and Paramount Pictures, 1987.

[113] Garcia, Paul, Jr. Interview by Debra Murphy. Transcript, The Veterans History Project, The Library of Congress, Washington, DC.

In Richard Slotkin's article "Unit Pride: Ethnic Platoons and the Myths of American Nationality," he surmises that during the boom of Vietnam War films there was a raised interest in class, racial, and ethnic differences.[114] In films that actually included Hispanic characters like Oliver Stone's *Platoon* and Stanley Kubrick's *Full Metal Jacket* the directors sought to demonstrate the differences between "street" minorities and more working-class or middle-class minorities. Slotkin presents a valid point in stating that these films want to pick at the differences between race and class in the Vietnam War, however these films do not give depth to Hispanic characters and they do not allow Hispanic characters to be heroes. The actions that some of these Chicano and Hispanic characters perform in these Vietnam War films are not heroic or extraordinary, because the writers and the directors of these films do not desire to upstage the European-American hero.

In the dialogue of examining films in which Chicanos and other Hispanics have participated in regarding the Vietnam War Randall Wallace's *We Were*

---

[114] Richard Slotkin, "Unit Pride: Ethnic Platoons and the Myths of American Nationality," *American Literary History* 13, no. 3 (Autumn, 2001): 491.

Soldiers must be mentioned. This 2002 film was based on the novel by Lt. Gen. Harold G. Moore and Joseph L. Galloway titled *We Were Soldiers Once... And Young*. The film is a reenactment of the Battle of the Ia Drang Valley of 1965 and tells the story of a platoon that gets pinned down in a hot landing zone.[115] The platoon is led by Lt. Colonel Hal Moore who is played by Mel Gibson. The main characters of the platoon are Sgt. Maj. Basil L. Plumley, 2nd Lt. Jack Geoghegan, Maj. Bruce Crandall, and Captain Tony Nadal.[116] Captain Tony Nadal who was played by Jsu Garcia is the only character in the film who is Hispanic. In comparison with other films who use the Vietnam War as their subject matter such as *The Deer Hunter*, and *Hamburger Hill* this is a giant leap forward in the direction of ethnic equality, however when the platoon is compared with the amount of Chicanos and Hispanics who served in the Battle of the Ia Drang Valley the percentage is quite low. However the book that Moore and Galloway wrote included many more Hispanics and Chicanos than the film

---

[115] Randall Wallace, *We Were Soldiers*, DVD, Icon Productions and Paramount Pictures, 2002.

[116] Ibid.

did. For example the book chronicles the death of Sergeant Agustin Chavez Paredez a Chicano from Big Springs, Texas who fought valiantly and who gave his life for the effort against communism in Landing Zone Albany of the Ia Drang Valley.[117] Sgt. Paredez was one of many Chicanos and Hispanics that participated in the Battle of the Ia Drang Valley but as with many other Hispanics his sacrifices are not remembered through any representation in Hollywood films.

Since Mexican-Americans are both European and Native American they are perceived by mainstream American society as different and possibly suspicious. Many Chicanos also speak Spanish as well as English or demonstrate strong ties to other social customs that are part of historic traditions. Most Mexican-Americans adhere to the doctrines of Catholicism and not Protestantism as most of Americans do. All of these notions differentiate Chicanos and Hispanics from the hegemonic American culture, and as a consequence racism manifests itself towards Chicanos. Hollywood however is a unique case

[117] Ia Drang Valley Memorial on the Virtual Wall, "Agustin Chavez Paredez," http://www.virtualwall.org/dp/ParedezAC01a.htm (accessed December 7, 2012).

because as other Americans become more open to understanding and even accepting Americans of different ethnic and racial groups the film companies remain trapped in bigotry. Even today film companies and producers claim to be multi-cultural and accepting of actors and characters that are different, but in fact veil racism behind a blanket of token-ness.

Chicanos mostly seem to be cast in films as landscapers, maids, nannies, gang-bangers, or drug-dealers. It is a manner in which Hollywood producers and directors attempt to maintain their ethnic hegemony over every other racial and ethnic group. In other words if Chicanos and Hispanics are always represented in negative roles or as the "bad guys" society will perceive them as such and never believe that they could be heroes, scientists, doctors, professors, or Vietnam War veterans. The truth is that in life outside of the silver screen Chicanos and Hispanics have embodied all of these professions, and it is no surprise to find a Hispanic or Mexican-American scientist, engineer, doctor, police officer, teacher, or soldier.

The idea of using film and television to continue reciprocating racist attitudes can be interpreted as propaganda. The same producers and directors in Hollywood that perpetuate this sort of racist propaganda also claim to create a sense of unity in America by arguing that they are "color blind." Laura Pulido describes this idea of color blindness as a method in which people can continue to be white-supremacists and racial bigots, but not have to be inconvenienced or give up any privileges in order to achieve racial or ethnic equality.[118] When films like *Platoon*, *We Were Soldiers*, and *Full Metal Jacket* insert one or two Hispanic characters minimally into the plot this creates the sense that these films are being inclusive and color blind. In practice however and after deep analysis it can be inferred that the directors, writers, and producers are merely practicing the token-ness method of making the film appear to be inclusive. The Hispanic soldiers do not contribute intelligent conversations, heroic actions, or even demonstrate complex emotional attitudes. They are instead one-dimensional and are written out of the plot or made out to be the background for the other actors. These practices do not have any logical reasoning because

[118] Laura Pulido, "Rethinking Environmental Racism: White Privilege and Urban Development in Southern California," *Annals of the Association of American Geographers* 90, no. 1 (March, 2000): 15.

of how truly complex the Chicano soldier's experience during the Vietnam War era was.   Chicanos during this period were struggling to find durable employment and recognition as first-class American citizens, and this can be witnessed through analyzing Cesar Chavez's and the United Farmworkers of America's struggle with obtaining workers' rights for agricultural workers. Mexican-Americans were also fighting issues of discrimination that they were experiencing by federal and state governments in obtaining an education and discriminatory draft boards. These issues culminated in the Mexican-American Civil Rights marches of southern California and the Chicano Moratoriums for drafting Chicanos disproportionately into the military. The Hollywood filmmakers seem to ignore all of these issues that affected Chicanos during this period, and pretend that they never occurred so that they do not have to cast Hispanic characters into these films. When they are casted into these films they are usually just a token character that dies off quickly or is expendable.

In conclusion Chicano characters in Vietnam War films need more depth, and their characters need to be involved in the plot more so than they have been.

Hollywood producers and writers must demonstrate that the Hispanic ethnic group is an important part of the American population or else the argument that Hollywood uses discriminatory practices against Chicanos, Hispanics, and Latinos will never be able to be disproven. In order for Vietnam War films to be a model of respect for the sacrifices that Vietnam veterans gave to the effort against communism more ethnicities should be represented in these theatrical manifestations.

References

Garcia, Paul, Jr. Interview by Debra Murphy. Transcript, The Veterans History Project, The Library of Congress, Washington, DC.

Ia Drang Valley Memorial on the Virtual Wall. "Agustin Chavez Paredez." http://www.virtualwall.org/dp/ParedezAC01a.htm (accessed December 7, 2012).

Irvin, John. *Hamburger Hill*. DVD. RKO Pictures and Paramount Pictures, 1987.

Kubrick, Stanley. *Full Metal Jacket*. DVD. Harrier Films and Warner Bros. Pictures, 1987.

Pulido, Laura. "Rethinking Environmental Racism: White Privilege and Urban Development in Southern California." *Annals of the Association of American Geographers* 90, no. 1 (March, 2000): 12-40.

Slotkin, Richard. "Unit Pride: Ethnic Platoons and the Myths of American Nationality." *American Literary History* 13, no. 3 (Autumn, 2001): 469-498.

Stone, Oliver. *Platoon*. DVD. Hemdale Film Corporation and Orion Pictures, 1986.

Wallace, Randall. *We Were Soldiers*. DVD. Icon Productions and Paramount Pictures, 2002.

Wayne, John, Ray Kellogg, and Mervyn LeRoy. *The Green Berets*. DVD. Warner Bros. and Seven Arts, 1968.

Bibliography

Chapter One

Anzaldúa, Gloria E. *Borderlands/La Frontera: The New Mestiza*. San Francisco, CA: Aunt Lute Books, 1987.

Cutler, John Alba. "Disappeared Men: Chicana/o Authenticity and the American War in Viet Nam." *American Literature* no. 3, vol. 81 (September 2009): 583-611.

Dominguez, Gil. *They Answered the Call: Latinos in the Vietnam War*. Baltimore, MD: Publish America, 2004.

Gartner, Scott Sigmund and Gary M. Segura. "Race, Casualties, and Opinion in the Vietnam War." *The Journal of Politics* no. 1, vol. 62 (February 2000): 115-146.

Mariscal, George. *Aztlán and Viet Nam: Chicano and Chicana Experiences of the War*. Berkeley, CA: University of California Press, 1999.

Oropeza, Lorena. *Raza Si! Guerra No! Chicano Protest and Patriotism During the Viet Nam War Era.* Berkeley, CA: University of California Press, 2005.

Ramirez, Juan. *A Patriot After All: the Story of a Chicano Vietnam Vet.* Albuquerque, NM: University of New Mexico Press, 1999.

Trujillo, Charley. *Soldados: Chicanos in Viet Nam.* San Jose, CA: Chusma House Publications, 1990.

Ybarra, Lea. *Vietnam Veteranos: Chicanos Recall the War.* Austin, TX: University of Texas Press, 2004.

Young, Crawford. *The Rising Tide of Cultural Pluralism: The Nation-State at Bay?* Madison, WI: The University of Wisconsin Press, 1993.

Chapter Two

Brush, Peter. "Higher and Higher: American Drug Use in Vietnam."*Vietnam*, December 2002, http://www.library.vanderbilt.edu/central/Brush/American-drug-use-vietnam.htm (accessed February 3, 2013).

Bustamante, Antonio P. 2010. Interview by Debbie Lopez. March 7. Transcript, Veterans History Project, The Library of Congress, Washington, DC.

Cisneros, Sandra. *Woman Hollering Creek and Other Stories*. New York, NY: Vintage/Random House, 1992.

Dominguez, Gil. *They Answered the Call: Latinos in the Vietnam War*. Baltimore, MD: Publish America, 2004.

García, Mario T., and Sal Castro, *Blowout! Sal Castro & the Chicano Struggle for Educational Justice*. Chapel Hill, NC: The University of North Carolina Press, 2011.

Garcia, Ralph. 2002. Interview by Philip Shaull. December 17. Transcript, Veterans History Project, The Library of Congress, Washington, DC.

Hunt, Michael H., ed. *A Vietnam War Reader: A Documentary from American and Vietnamese Perspectives*. Chapel Hill, NC: The University of North Carolina Press, 2010.

Huntington, Samuel P. "The Hispanic Challenge." *Foreign Policy* no. 141 (March-April 2004): 30-45.

Jacobs, Seth. *America's Miracle Man in Vietnam: Ngo Dinh Diem, Religion, Race, and U.S. Intervention in*

Southeast Asia, 1950-1957. Durham, NC: Duke
University Press, 2004.

Jauregui, Joaquin M. 2009. Interview by Efrain Avila.
March 11. Transcript, Veterans History Project, The
Library of Congress, Washington, DC.

Kirkwood, Burton. *The History of Mexico*. Westport, CT:
Greenwood Press, 2000.

Lenin, Vladimir Ilich. *Essay on Religion by Lenin.*
Forgotten Books, 2012.

Lopez, Luis Muñiz. 2009. Interview by William L.
Browne. August 7. Transcript, Veterans History
Project, The Library of Congress, Washington, DC.

Mason, Leslie. "The Conflict Between Communism and
Religion." *The Communist Review* (2007),
http://www.marxists.org/history/international/comin
tern/sections/britain/periodicals/communist_review/
1924/02/mason.htm (accessed January 3, 2013).

Merton, Thomas. *Conjectures of a Guilty Bystander*.
Garden City, NY: Doubleday & Company,   Inc.,
1968.

---. "Note for Ave Maria," *Passion for Peace: The Social Essays*, ed. William H. Shannon. New York, NY: The Crossroad Publishing Company, 1997.

Mini, John. *The Aztec Virgin: The Secret Mystical Tradition of Our Lady of Guadalupe.* Sausalito, CA: Trans-Hyperborean Institute of Science, 2000.

Montano, Bobby J. 2011. Interview by Rachel Trujillo. October 26. Transcript, Veterans History Project, The Library of Congress, Washington, DC.

Montoya, Abran F., Jr. 2002. Interview by Dena R. Montoya Osborn. December 7. Transcript, Veterans History Project, The Library of Congress, Washington, DC.

National Archives. "School Desegregation and Civil Rights Stories: Orange County, California." http://www.archives.gov/philadelphia/education/des egregation/orange-county.html (accessed January 21, 2013).

Nelson, Michael ed. *The Evolving Presidency: Addresses, Cases, Essays, Letters, Reports, Resolutions, Transcripts, and Other Landmark Documents,*

1787-1998. Washington, DC: Congressional
Quarterly Inc., 1999.

Oropeza, Lorena. *¡Raza Si! ¡Guerra No! Chicano Protest
and Patriotism During the Viet Nam War Era.*
Berkeley, CA: University of California Press, 2005.

Ramirez, Juan. *A Patriot After All: the Story of a Chicano
Vietnam Vet.* Albuquerque, NM: University of New
Mexico Press, 1999.

Rhee, Sonya and Charley Trujillo. *Discussion Guide:
Soldados Chicanos in Viet Nam.* Arlington, VA:
Public Broadcasting Service, 2003.

Rodriguez, Louis. 2005. Interview by Debra Murphy. July
28. Transcript, Veterans History Project, The
Library of Congress, Washington, DC.

Texas State Historical Association. "Segregation."
http://www.tshaonline.org/handbook/online/articles/
pks01 (accessed January 20, 2013).

The Vietnam Center and Archive. "Vietnam Archive
Robert S. McNamara Resources."
http://www.vietnam.ttu.edu/resources/mcnamara/
(accessed February 1, 2013).

Trujillo, Charley. *Soldados: Chicanos in Viet Nam*. San Jose, CA: Chusma House Publications, 1990.

U.S. Department of Defense. *Melvin R. Laird*, Secretary of Defense Histories. Washington, DC, 2012.

U.S.Department of Veterans Affairs. *Veterans' Diseases Associated With Agent Orange*. Washington, DC, 2012.

Willbanks, James H. *The Tet Offensive: A Concise History*. New York, NY: Columbia University Press, 2007.

Ybarra, Lea. *Vietnam Veteranos: Chicanos Recall the War*. Austin, TX: University of Texas Press, 2004.

Chapter Three

Garcia, Paul, Jr. Interview by Debra Murphy. Transcript, The Veterans History Project, The Library of Congress, Washington, DC.

Ia Drang Valley Memorial on the Virtual Wall. "Agustin Chavez Paredez." http://www.virtualwall.org/dp/ParedezAC01a.htm (accessed December 7, 2012).

Irvin, John. *Hamburger Hill*. DVD. RKO Pictures and Paramount Pictures, 1987.

Kubrick, Stanley. *Full Metal Jacket*. DVD. Harrier Films and Warner Bros. Pictures, 1987.

Pulido, Laura. "Rethinking Environmental Racism: White Privilege and Urban Development in Southern California." *Annals of the Association of American Geographers* 90, no. 1 (March, 2000): 12-40.

Slotkin, Richard. "Unit Pride: Ethnic Platoons and the Myths of American Nationality." *American Literary History* 13, no. 3 (Autumn, 2001): 469-498.

Stone, Oliver. *Platoon*. DVD. Hemdale Film Corporation and Orion Pictures, 1986.

Wallace, Randall. *We Were Soldiers*. DVD. Icon Productions and Paramount Pictures, 2002.

Wayne, John, Ray Kellogg, and Mervyn LeRoy. *The Green Berets*. DVD. Warner Bros. and Seven Arts, 1968.

About The Author

Juan "John" C. Trejo lives in Atlanta with his wife Lorena. He holds a B.A. in History and an M.A. in American Studies from Kennesaw State University. He specializes in American History of the 20th Century with a major focus on the Chicano experience. This is his second published book, his first book *Revolutionary Minds of the Vietnam War Era* was published in 2012.

Made in the USA
Las Vegas, NV
05 September 2022

54745879R00081